MRT-GEN

D1479574

Development Co-operation Review Series

Denmark

1995 No. 10

Development Assistance Committee

Université d'Ottawa
BIBLIOTHÈQUES
LIBRARIES
University of Ottawa

ORGANISATION FOR ECONOMIC CO-OPERATION AND DEVELOPMENT

ORGANISATION FOR ECONOMIC CO-OPERATION AND DEVELOPMENT

Pursuant to Article 1 of the Convention signed in Paris on 14th December 1960, and which came into force on 30th September 1961, the Organisation for Economic Co-operation and Development (OECD) shall promote policies designed :

— to achieve the highest sustainable economic growth and employment and a rising standard of living in Member countries, while maintaining financial stability, and thus to contribute to the development of the world economy;

— to contribute to sound economic expansion in Member as well as non-member countries in the process of economic development; and

— to contribute to the expansion of world trade on a multilateral, non-discriminatory basis in accordance with international obligations.

The original Member countries of the OECD are Austria, Belgium, Canada, Denmark, France, Germany, Greece, Iceland, Ireland, Italy, Luxembourg, the Netherlands, Norway, Portugal, Spain, Sweden, Switzerland, Turkey, the United Kingdom and the United States. The following countries became Members subsequently through accession at the dates indicated hereafter: Japan (28th April 1964), Finland (28th January 1969), Australia (7th June 1971), New Zealand (29th May 1973) and Mexico (18th May 1994). The Commission of the European Communities takes part in the work of the OECD (Article 13 of the OECD Convention).

In order to achieve its aims the OECD has set up a number of specialised committees. One of these is the Development Assistance Committee, whose Members have agreed to secure an expansion of aggregate volume of resources made available to developing countries and to improve their effectiveness. To this end, Members periodically review together both the amount and the nature of their contributions to aid programmes, bilateral and multilateral, and consult each other on all other relevant aspects of their development assistance policies.

The Members of the Development Assistance Committee are Australia, Austria, Belgium, Canada, Denmark, Finland, France, Germany, Ireland, Italy, Japan, Luxembourg, the Netherlands, New Zealand, Norway, Portugal, Spain, Sweden, Switzerland, the United Kingdom, the United States and the Commission of the European Communities.

Publié en français sous le titre :

SÉRIE DES EXAMENS EN MATIÈRE DE COOPÉRATION POUR LE DÉVELOPPEMENT :

DANEMARK

© OECD 1995

Applications for permission to reproduce or translate all or part of this publication should be made to:

Head of Publications Service, OECD

2, rue André-Pascal, 75775 PARIS CEDEX 16, France.

HC
360
.E44
D45
1995

Foreword

The Development Assistance Committee (DAC) conducts periodic reviews to improve the individual and collective development co-operation efforts of DAC Members. The policies and efforts of individual Members are critically examined approximately once every three years. Some seven programmes are examined annually.

The peer review is prepared by the Secretariat. The country under review provides a memorandum setting out the main developments in its policies and programmes and the Secretariat visits the capital to interview officials, parliamentarians, and NGO representatives of the donor country to obtain a first-hand insight into the current issues surrounding the development co-operation efforts of the Member concerned. Brief field visits investigate how Members have absorbed the major DAC principles and concerns and examine operations in recipient countries, particularly with regard to sustainability, environment, women in development, participatory development, and local aid co-ordination.

Putting all this information and analysis together, the Secretariat prepares a draft report on the Member's development co-operation which is the basis for the DAC review meeting at which senior officials from the Member under review discuss a series of questions posed in a brief document: "Main issues for the Review". These questions are formulated by the Secretariat in association with officials from two other DAC Members acting as "examiners", who have also visited the donor capital to investigate trends and issues in the programme. The main discussion points and operational policy recommendations emerging from the review meeting are set out in the Summary and Conclusions section of the publication.

This publication contains the Summary and Conclusions as agreed by the Committee following the review on 31 May 1995 in Paris and the Report prepared by the Secretariat for the DAC's Review of the development co-operation policies of Denmark. The report is published on the authority of the Secretary-General of the OECD.

James Michel
DAC Chair

List of Acronyms

AfDB	African Development Bank
AsDB	Asian Development Bank
BoP	Balance of payments
CMC	Committee for Mixed Credits
DAC	Development Assistance Committee
DANIDA	Danish International Development Agency[1]
DBP	Development Bank of the Philippines
DEF	Danish Export Finance Corporation
DIPO	Danish Import Promotion Office
FAO	Food and Agriculture Organisation of the United Nations
GNP	Gross national product
GOI	Government of India
IDA	International Development Association
IFU*	Danish Investment Promotion Agency
LLDCs	Least developed countries
MFA	Ministry of Foreign Affairs
MS*	Mellemfolkeligt Samvirke
NGO	Non-governmental organisation
ODA	Official development assistance
SRHR	Sexual and Reproductive Health and Rights
TANWA	Tamil Nadu Women in Agriculture
UN	United Nations
UNCED	United Nations Conference on Environment and Development
UNCTAD	United Nations Conference on Trade and Development
UNDDSMS	United Nations Department for Development Support and Management Services
UNDP	United Nations Development Programme
UNESCO	United Nations Educational, Scientific and Cultural Organisation
UNFPA	United Nations Fund for Population
UNICEF	United Nations Children's Fund

---

* Denotes acronym in original language.
1. The Agency ceased formally to exist in 1991, its functions being taken over by the South Group in the Ministry of Foreign Affairs.

Table of Contents

Graphs

Boxes

Charts

Summary and Conclusions

Aid policy orientations

Denmark is now in the second year of the 1994 strategy *"A Developing World – Strategy for Danish Development Policy towards the Year 2000"* (the Strategy). Building on the 1989 Plan of Action for Danish development co-operation, the Strategy aims at adjusting Danish policies to the new global situation and at further improving coherence among these policies. While confirming fundamental and cross-cutting themes of Danish development co-operation, such as poverty alleviation, women in development, environment and good government, the Strategy introduces population, trade and debt relief as additional priority themes. To improve the effectiveness of aid, the Strategy envisages a concentration of official development assistance (ODA) on a limited number of recipient countries and on international aid organisations whose programmes correspond most to Danish aid priorities. To improve policy guidance for development co-operation, the Danish Prime Minister appointed a Minister for Development Co-operation in 1993.

In January 1995, an opinion poll by the Gallup Institute revealed that three-quarters of the Danish population support the principle that Denmark's aid volume should equal 1 per cent of gross national product (GNP). There are some particular features which distinguish the Danish aid system from others and contribute to its positive image with the public. One of these elements is the strong involvement of all components of Danish society in the conception of aid policy, and also in its implementation. Non-governmental organisations (NGOs), consultancy firms, researchers, trade unions and the private business community form the so-called "Danish Resource Base" for the aid programme.

Bilateral assistance

A new and promising feature of Danish assistance is the participation of recipient country administrations and target groups in both the conception and the implementation of programmes supported by Denmark. The fact that Danish and other expatriate experts do not normally act as programme managers, but as behind-the-scene advisors, reinforces the "ownership" dimension for aid recipients. At the same time, however, a strong presence of aid specialists at the field level ensures that advice is available at all stages of the programme cycle, including help in overcoming bureaucratic hurdles in local administrations.

Denmark has completed the selection of 20 programme countries on which most of bilateral assistance will be concentrated in future. Except for one country, they are all in the low-income category, including eleven least developed countries. For a number of other countries, who in the past had regularly received official Danish assistance, direct official aid will be gradually phased out by 1999. The aid administration is now in the process of formulating new strategies – or revising existing ones – for each of the programme countries. The process starts with inviting local experts to draft analytical papers on the country's situation and needs and proceeds through consultations involving local partners and the Danish "resource base". In addition to focusing support for each programme country on a few sectors where Danish support is likely to be most effective, this process is expected to reinforce local engagement in development co-operation.

Multilateral co-operation

Another new concept emerging from the Strategy concerns Denmark's participation in international organisations. Denmark intends moving further from the principle of financial burden-sharing, via established contribution patterns, towards a concept of selective support for institutions whose activities are of high quality and correspond to priority areas as defined by Denmark. This approach, based on Danish efforts to assess and improve the efficiency and effectiveness of international institutions, could be termed "active multilateralism". Danish authorities would be willing, on a case-by-case basis, to provide financial support that is higher than Denmark's assessed share, such as is presently the case for the United Nations Development Programme (UNDP), for which Denmark is the third largest contributor. This does not mean that Denmark is ready to fill gaps in budgets of institutions resulting from diminished support or withdrawal by other Member countries.

Danish resource base

The Strategy recommends establishing closer links between the Danish aid authorities and civil society including, as noted above, the preparation of country strategies. While most NGO activities in developing countries are fully funded from the aid budget, Danish NGOs are said to act rather independently from government. The complementarity between NGO programmes and official Danish aid may need to be clarified further as the new country strategies emerge. Another initiative concerns the promotion of partnerships between private sector professionals and institutions in programme countries and Denmark through twinning arrangements.

New guidelines on aid financed procurement were adopted in September 1994. Without abandoning the aim of 50 per cent of bilateral ODA to be spent in Denmark, the guidelines rendered aid financed procurement more flexible. As a result, local companies in recipient countries should become more involved as suppliers.

Aid policy and management

In mid-1991, the South Group of the Ministry of Foreign Affairs (MFA) became responsible for Denmark's policies in the areas of multilateral and bilateral co-operation. In bilateral relations, aid, trade and general foreign policy are all the responsibility of the South Group. A Minister for Development Co-operation in the Ministry provides guidance for the conception and implementation of these policies. Since one single ministry is responsible for these major issues, the Danish authorities have not yet felt the need to create an interministerial co-ordinating body to ensure policy coherence with regard to development co-operation. However, an interministerial committee regularly co-ordinates on a range of development issues arising in the European Union context.

Country programming and decentralised management

The selection of the final programme countries in 1994 brought the process of concentration for Denmark's bilateral aid programme a step forward. Further steps are required to complete this transition. First, for most programme countries, specific strategies need to be formulated. This process takes time, as Denmark has adopted a participatory approach. Second, the winding up of earlier programmes for regular aid recipients will take until 1999. By then, the implementation phase will have almost run its course. While programme countries will receive the bulk of bilateral ODA once the concentration process has been completed, the Danish programme has earmarked funding for aid in special sectoral and policy areas for which all developing countries are eligible. These are essentially: support for democratisation and human rights; Danish NGO projects; and the provision of mixed credits for credit-worthy countries. Given that programme countries are also eligible for assistance in these areas, there would seem to be a need to define more clearly the role of these types of aid in country programming.

The 1989 Plan of Action advocated a policy of decentralisation by transferring responsibility for development co-operation to Danish Embassies in developing countries. The implementation of this policy is dependent upon the availability of sufficient numbers of competent staff. In this context it is worth noting that the field management of Danish aid has been substantially reinforced over the past few years, after the restructuring of the MFA. The general policy framework for co-operation with a given recipient is determined by the MFA, based on an extensive dialogue with the Government and other actors in the recipient countries and with the Danish resource base. Field staff accomplish a major share of the preparatory work for country programming and most of the monitoring of project implementation.

As a result of the move in Danish bilateral assistance towards sector programmes and support for decentralised public sector activities in its programme countries, there is a need for increased participation of middle- and lower-level local administrations in the preparation and implementation of development programmes. Since the capacity for these tasks is often lacking, Denmark provides technical and financial assistance to a number of its programme countries for improving public sector institutional capacity, *e.g.* Nepal, Nicaragua, Zambia and Uganda. In the specific area of aid management and accountability, Denmark has supported the United Nations Department for Development Support and Management Services (UNDDSMS) in the development of a ''Framework for Harmonized Aid Management and Accountability''.

Assessment of results

An Evaluation Unit in the South Group, which is independent of aid programme management, is increasingly assessing the effects of Danish aid on particular sectors and on the development of specific recipient countries. Thematic evaluations were carried out in 1993 and 1994, covering balance-of-payments (BoP) support, women in development, cofinancing and NGO activities. In 1994, a major study of Danish BoP support concluded that in its present form – tied commodity import financing – this aid is not always appropriate to the objectives sought, in particular in the context of structural adjustment. Denmark is among the few Development Assistance Committee (DAC) Members who have begun to monitor and evaluate the effectiveness of multilateral aid institutions at both recipient country level and in general.

Aid volume and areas of assistance

In 1992, Denmark achieved an aid volume performance of 1 per cent of GNP, an objective which had been formulated by Parliament seven years earlier. In 1993, Denmark ranked first among DAC Member countries in this respect, with an ODA/GNP ratio of 1.03 per cent, and $1.3 billion of ODA. In 1994, Danish ODA amounted to $1.5 billion, again corresponding to 1.03 per cent of GNP. Multilateral co-operation plays an important role in the Danish aid programme. International organisations receive a relatively large share of Danish ODA, amounting to 44 per cent in 1993 and 45 per cent in 1994.

Over 90 per cent of Denmark's bilateral ODA is traditionally reserved for poor countries in Africa and Asia (least developed and other low-income countries). While for 1992/93 this ratio was confirmed by official statistics, the significant amount of unallocated bilateral aid – one-third of the total – renders these statistics less meaningful. The sector of "social infrastructure and services" was the focus of bilateral assistance in 1992/93. Over 40 per cent of bilateral aid was used for such programmes, as compared to only 15 per cent five years earlier. This emphasis on the social area contrasts sharply with the performance of other DAC Members – the DAC average was 21 per cent in 1992/93 – but no bilateral Danish funds have been provided for direct measures in the area of population. It is Danish policy to integrate support for this area in assistance for the health sector.

Another new area for assistance is being addressed through the Private Sector Development Programme of 1993. By establishing closer contacts between Danish industry and enterprises in developing countries the aim is to facilitate the transfer of technology and know-how and improve access by Danish firms to markets in developing countries, both through exports and joint ventures. The programme has been launched on a pilot basis, and will be reviewed in 1995. It is linked to other programmes and institutions with which the Danish resource base is involved: the mixed credit programme; foreign direct investment promotion by the Danish Investment Promotion Agency (IFU); and assisting developing countries' exports through the Danish Import Promotion Office (DIPO).

The Committee discussed Denmark's policy and practice of aid tying. Although an overall target ratio of bilateral ODA is set for procurement in Denmark, individual aid transactions are reported as being in principle untied. The DAC discussed how the effective untying of aid in the context of DAC rules and disciplines could be achieved, and how transparency in Danish policy and practices could be improved. The DAC looks forward to responses from the Danish authorities in the course of its current work on these issues.

Conclusion

Danish development co-operation inspires confidence and optimism in the public mind, not only in Denmark, but elsewhere as well. The programme's achievements and efficiency could help to dispel confusion and cynicism regarding the role of aid and its effectiveness. While the programme has encountered the same challenges as other aid programmes in adapting to the new political and economic perspectives since the late 1980s, the decisions on policy change in the case of Denmark seem to have been more radical and more timely than in other donor countries. Earlier efforts to improve the coherence of Danish policies towards developing countries probably helped in this process. But above all, it is the care being taken to maximise the effectiveness of the Danish contribution in terms of the specific development needs and institutional capacities of each programme country that is the fundamental strength of Danish development co-operation. This strength should be maintained and safeguarded.

Chapter I

Aid Policy Orientations

The act governing Danish development co-operation was passed by Parliament in 1971. It states two principal objectives of Denmark's official development assistance to developing countries: first, support for their efforts to achieve economic growth, through co-operation with these countries' governments and authorities, as a contribution to social progress and political independence, and, second, promotion of mutual understanding and solidarity through cultural co-operation. In the latter area, about $1 million was spent in 1993 in support of publishing and distributing African literature in Africa and in Europe, including Denmark.

A Plan of Action for Danish development co-operation, adopted by Parliament in 1989, has brought about changes in certain areas. While corroborating the overall objectives for Denmark's development co-operation and the basically equal distribution of the aid programme on bilateral and multilateral channels, the Plan has improved the flexibility in ODA financed procurement through an ''informal tying'' device; introduced a full grant system in bilateral co-operation; stressed the importance of support for developing countries' structural adjustment; enlarged the group of recipient programme countries to 25; and, finally, increased decentralised aid management through further transfer of responsibilities and staff from Headquarters to Danish Embassies. The 1989 Plan of Action also mentions human rights as one of several cross-cutting issues in development co-operation. In this regard, Denmark has taken action in recent years, either through specific assistance or through the reduction of aid in cases of persistent inadequate performance by the recipient authorities in the human rights area (*e.g.* Kenya).

A. Strategy towards the Year 2000

In March 1994, the Government presented to Parliament a 100 page study: *''A Developing World – Strategy for Danish Development Policy towards the Year 2000''*. It was endorsed by consensus in Parliament as a successor to the 1989 Plan of Action. The Strategy states that overall objectives of Danish aid are being maintained and that the ODA volume will remain at 1 per cent of GNP. The changes in international relations that have occurred since 1989 form the point of departure for the new Strategy. There is an awareness on the part of the Danish authorities that forms and content of assistance must be adjusted continuously, both in recipient countries and in Denmark, in order to remain relevant and effective. The Strategy emphasizes that development co-operation must be part of the broader frame of Danish foreign policy, including trade and environment. The first chapter provides the general perspective for Denmark's development assistance, identifying the cross-cutting themes of poverty alleviation, a stronger role of women in development, environmentally sustainable development and the promotion of democratisation. Another five chapters of the Strategy cover bilateral co-operation, multilateral co-operation, emergency assistance, priority themes and co-operation with the Danish resource base (research institutes, NGOs, general public, the enterprise sector). A brief overview of these chapters is provided below. Given the relatively ambitious goals set by the Strategy, the Danish aid authorities intend to be particularly attentive to its effective implementation and plan to review the actual fulfilment of development objectives in 1997. It can be expected that in this exercise the views of Danish private aid institutions will be taken into account.

Bilateral co-operation

The strategic objective in this area is to concentrate co-operation on 20 recipient countries, essentially in the form of sector assistance. For each programme country a special strategy will be formulated, limiting Danish assistance to a few selected sectors where it is likely to be most effective.

Multilateral co-operation

For Danish participation in multilateral co-operation, a new concept is also emerging from the Strategy. While still underlining the need for better financial burden-sharing among donors, Denmark intends in future to move to a much greater extent towards selectively supporting international institutions whose activities are of high quality and correspond to priority areas as defined by Denmark. This process of selection is based on assessments of efficiency and effectiveness of relevant institutions, which Denmark undertakes alone or jointly with other donors. Under the new concept, which has been termed "active multilateralism", the Danish authorities would be willing, on a case-by-case basis, to provide a volume of financial support that is higher than Denmark's assessed share. The concept does not imply, however, that Denmark is generally prepared to fill gaps in budgets of institutions from which other members have withdrawn.

Emergency assistance

The Strategy spells out the need for relating short-term emergency relief more closely to long-term development co-operation. Several options to achieve this goal are mentioned: in the case of long lasting crisis situations, traditional emergency relief should be transformed into more general assistance, including for the restructuring of social conditions; relief organisations should be encouraged to develop programmes in the grey area between emergency relief and long-term assistance, which is presently hardly covered by aid programmes; finally, Denmark pledges support for an "international humanitarian capacity", composed of volunteers with professional background who can be deployed at short notice to assist in Danish or international relief actions.

Priority themes

Population, trade and debt relief are the areas singled out by the Strategy as requiring particular Danish support. A sector strategy was formulated in 1994 for assistance in the population area. In the trade area Denmark intends to promote, among other things, coherence between European development co-operation and trade and agricultural policies of the European Union. Regarding indebtedness, Denmark will help to alleviate debt of its programme countries to international institutions, either by financial contributions to multilateral debt relief arrangements, or by financing debt service payments directly through bilateral ODA.

Co-operation with the Danish resource base

The Strategy recommends establishing closer links between the Danish aid authorities and civil society to the extent that it is involved in aid matters (the "Danish Resource Base"). In this context, it is suggested that interested parties from the business and NGO sectors should become involved in the preparation of country strategies. It is also suggested that the participation of the civil resource base in Danish development co-operation be intensified by promoting partnerships between professions and institutions in programme countries and Denmark (twinning arrangements).

B. Trend towards concentration of bilateral assistance

Components of bilateral assistance

The guiding principle of the Strategy is to increase the efficiency and effectiveness of Danish aid. To achieve this, Danish bilateral ODA is to be concentrated on a limited number of recipients ("programme countries"), and in each of these on a few sectors. For all programme countries, particular country strategies will have to be formulated. The first objective of the new bilateral strategy has been fulfilled: the selection of 20 programme countries has been completed in discussions between the aid administration and the Danish resource base. In this process, aid programmes for 18 other developing countries have been phased out or will be phased out by 1999 (China, Thailand, etc.). Three other recipients have been added in 1994 to the Group of programme countries (Bolivia, Ethiopia, Niger). Countries in this category receive assistance in grant form from the budget line for programme countries, administered by the regional departments in the MFA.

While the bulk of aid funding is reserved for programme countries, other recipients can also benefit from bilateral Danish ODA in special areas (see Chapter II, Section B). The fact that programme countries can receive assistance in these "special areas", *e.g.* under the associated financing scheme, raises the question of coherence between the special assistance and the country strategy. It is not clear whether this overlap actually helps to improve the impact of Danish aid, but it certainly gives Danish aid managers flexibility. However, Danish Embassies in programme countries play a co-ordinating role to ensure coherence.

The process of formulating new country strategies, or of revising existing ones, is presently underway. By mid-1995 such strategies were ready for four programme countries (India, Mozambique, Viet Nam and Zambia), as well as the strategy for transitional assistance to South Africa. In an innovative approach, the Danish authorities start this process by asking local groups in a programme country – NGOs, researchers, government representatives – to prepare a paper on the country's development needs which could be met by Denmark's assistance. These country papers serve as a basis for subsequent discussions in Denmark between the aid administration and the Danish resource base on which sectors to select, and on the overall shape of the country strategy. The selection of sectors for Danish assistance to any given programme country is closely related to, and indeed part of, the country strategy. However, difficulties can arise when the administration discusses the choice of sectors with the Danish resource base. The NGO community generally prefers aid to social sectors, while Danish enterprises plead for more infrastructure support. Similarly, in government-to-government negotiations, some recipient governments have difficulty in restricting their choice of Danish assistance to a few sectors, given the many areas in need of external support.

C. New approach to multilateral co-operation

For the Danish aid authorities, multilateral co-operation remains equal in terms of financial commitments to their bilateral efforts. Given the relatively large share of Danish aid (approximately half of the aid budget) being channelled through international organisations, Denmark is keen to ensure efficient and effective use of these funds. As for bilateral ODA, the Strategy therefore recommends that co-operation should concentrate on institutions whose activities correspond best to Danish aid objectives and complement them. Complementarity should be achieved in geographical distribution of aid, with multilateral assistance reaching recipient countries outside the limited circle of programme countries, and within individual programme countries, by ensuring coherence between activities financed by Danish bilateral and multilateral ODA in the same country.

In implementing these recommendations, Denmark will increasingly decide its financial contributions on the basis of performance of the institutions (results, administration and financial accountability). However, given that general financial contributions to international institutions [*e.g.* International Development Association (IDA)/ European Funds] are largely on an assessed basis, the new approach may primarily concern United Nations (UN) organisations. For the UNDP, Denmark has become the third largest contributor and seems intent on continuing this substantial support in view of the Programme's important role in the policy dialogue with developing countries. Nevertheless, the size of Danish support will depend on the results of an assessment of UNDP's central role for co-ordinating policies and activities of the UN system. For the United Nations Children's Fund (UNICEF) the level of the Danish financial contribution will, in future, also depend on ongoing efforts by the organisation and some of its members, including Denmark, to improve its record in areas such as capacity development in developing countries, and accountability of the Fund's management.

In order to ensure a broader international profile of Danish assistance, Denmark is considering the creation of a number of trust funds to enable international institutions to undertake work in priority areas and to increase their effectiveness.

D. Danish resource base and public opinion

The main components of the so-called "Danish Resource Base" for Denmark's development co-operation programme are private aid institutions (NGOs), the business community and research institutes.

Most activities of Danish NGOs in developing countries are now fully funded from the aid budget because the organisations collect only small contributions from their constituencies, which are partly used to finance small aid projects. Danish NGOs are nevertheless said to act rather independently from government instructions. The degree of their independence from official aid policy may, however, vary from case to case and may depend on whether an NGO is active in a Danish programme country where its activity should be complementary to the official country programme. NGOs working in other developing countries may be more flexible in determining the shape of their programmes. The degree of independence of NGO programmes from government instructions also varies between larger and smaller NGOs. While the largest Danish NGOs work under framework agreements with the government which provide the organisations with autonomy and responsibility for planning and implementing projects, smaller NGOs have to present individual project suggestions for which they request official funding. Although in general they support the present orientations of Denmark's aid policy, NGOs also criticise the use of some parts of Danish bilateral ODA. In the view of these organisations, too large a portion of the aid funds is used to advance Danish commercial interests. Examples cited are infrastructure support for Uganda (repair work at Entebbe airport), the new Private Sector Programme and the new Mixed Credit Programme through which some recipients, such as China, will receive more ODA than some programme countries. Some Danish NGOs hold the view that the objective of concentrating bilateral assistance on 20 core recipients cannot be reached in this manner. They cite the cases of Eritrea and Ethiopia, the most recent programme countries, for whom no, or only very little, bilateral ODA was committed in 1993 and 1994.

In 1993, a *"Strategy for DANIDA's Co-operation with NGOs"* was adopted by the aid authorities after discussions and negotiations with the NGO community. Aimed at simplifying management procedures for what has become a major component of Denmark's aid programme (see below), the new NGO strategy provides several new orientations. The large NGOs with framework agreements will be given greater operational responsibility for project selection and implementation. Disbursements to NGOs under such framework agreements amounted to $24 million in 1993, representing over 3 per cent of bilateral Danish ODA. Annual allocations under these agreements vary between $5 million and $19 million. Single project applications from smaller NGOs will be processed twice a year under simplified procedures and clearer criteria of approval, which will ease DANIDA's administrative burden. Official support for individual NGO projects was $43 million in 1993, or 6 per cent of bilateral ODA. Official financial support for NGOs is also being improved. While the Danish International Development Agency (DANIDA) will continue its contribution to the NGO administrative cost at a flat rate of 7 per cent, from January 1995 NGOs are no longer required to fund part of project expenses, (for which they formerly had to contribute 10 per cent). The professional dialogue between DANIDA and the NGOs has been expanded to include NGO participation in the formulation of DANIDA's sector and country strategies. This task may be rendered more difficult by the fact that there is still no co-ordinating body at national level for regular contacts between Danish NGOs and government.

Officially funded activities of Danish NGOs

$ million

	1992	1993
Bilateral development projects	76.0	76.2
Humanitarian aid	61.9	42.9
Volunteer programme	27.8	28.5
Other	15.7	13.3
Total	**181.4**	**160.9**
(As a percentage of ODA net disbursements)	(13.0)	(12.0)

The large NGOs with which DANIDA has a framework or a similar agreement, are being monitored closely as to their capacity to design and implement development projects successfully. This "capacity analysis" will in future be carried out regularly and will be the basis for negotiations on future framework agreements. One of these large private organisations is the Danish Association for International Co-operation (in Danish: *Mellemfolkeligt Samvirke,* MS). MS does not consider fund raising as a principal task for a private aid institution and focuses its efforts on informing the Danish population about development issues and combating poverty in developing countries in using a grassroots approach ("development by people"), with women as a special target group (see Box 1 below).

Regarding the Danish business community, a Committee on Industrialisation in Developing Countries was established in 1989 with a view to improving the co-operation of DANIDA with Danish business and trade unions. The Minister for Development Co-operation is chairing this committee which includes the leading representatives of industry, commerce, agriculture, and trade unions. Among other initiatives, the Committee has completed an analysis of ways and means to use Danish resources (personnel, goods, and services) effectively in development assistance. This work was carried out by working groups covering areas such as environment,

Box 1. Profile of a Private Danish Aid Institution: *Mellemfolkeligt Samvirke* **(MS)**

1. *Mellemfolkeligt Samvirke* (MS), also called the Danish Association for International Co-operation, is a non-governmental, non-profit organisation working in the field of development, international understanding and solidarity. Through development work in the South and information activities in the North, MS supports a self-reliant and people-centered process of participatory and sustainable development.

   More than 5 000 individuals and 100 organisations support the work of MS through their membership. They elect the General Assembly, which meets once a year with the purpose of adopting the policy guidelines and electing the board.

2. **Poverty orientation**

   Poverty orientation is the core of the Association's strategy. MS aims at supporting the poor and under-privileged, including the handicapped, the illiterate, landless people, single mothers, street children, among others. This strategy is based on four principles:

   a) Development by people

   Development must be self-reliant and based on people's participation. Economic improvements are necessary but economic progress must be linked to popular participation and respect for democratic norms and human rights.

   b) Gender orientation

   Women are identified as a special target group in the MS work. The goal is to secure equal opportunities for women and men.

   c) Environment and development

   MS raises environmental questions in domestic debates and policies, and ensures that South views are heard. In partner countries MS gives priority to long-term solutions that on the one hand preserve and restore the local environment and on the other hand ensure that poor people can survive and gradually improve their situation.

   d) Sustainable development

   Beyond the mere environmental/political aspects, MS wishes to ensure that MS supported activities can be continued after it has pulled out of a project. Consequently, MS sees itself more as an advisory body rather than as a manager in the co-operation process. Its task is to identify and support local human resources and initiatives and to contribute towards the development of self-management and responsibility.

3. **MS training centre**

   MS runs a Training Centre for Development Co-operation at Arusha in Tanzania. Future development workers undergo six weeks training in Africa orientation, communication skills, English and Swahili, before taking up their posts in seven countries in East Africa.

   East African development workers from MS partner organisations also can obtain training in English, social transformation and project management at the centre, often together with their Danish counterparts.

4. **Solidarity and information**

   Solidarity and information work in Denmark is decisive for creating a broad popular understanding and respect for other cultures, other societies, and in particular for development countries' problems.

   Apart from practical solidarity work in the developing countries, the MS participants from work camps, study trips and development workers are encouraged to broaden public information and knowledge about the world's under-privileged groups.

   MS has a publishing house, a library, and a documentation centre, and publishes a string of magazines to inform the Danish public about the development problems and challenges of countries in the South.

   Another area for domestic information and solidarity work within MS is related to refugees and immigrants. Wars, unrest or global recession force many people to seek refuge or work in Denmark. As in many other European countries, this frequently results in incidents of racism and clashes between the foreigners and the Danes.

energy, agriculture, and technology transfer. DANIDA is at present considering the results of this analysis with the establishment of the Private Sector Programme as one of the first consequences.

A poll of Danish public opinion on development assistance was conducted by the Gallup Institute in January 1995. Almost three-quarters of the poll population (those over the age of 13) were in support of the present high levels of Danish aid. A particularly high level of support was found among the electorate belonging to the left of the political spectrum and supporters of small parties in the centre. It is worth noting that public support for Danish aid has markedly risen from some 35 per cent of the Danish population in the mid-1960s to over 70 per cent in the 1990s, and that this evolution has taken place in parallel with a rapid increase of the aid budget.

This positive perception of the aid programme by the Danish population is doubtlessly due to a large extent to an efficient information programme by the Information Office in the South Group. While the office devotes the major part of its budget to publications on relevant issues and to sponsoring journalists, a large number of NGOs also receive financial support for their information projects in Denmark. In addition, grants are provided for travel between Denmark and developing countries.

Chapter II

Aid Policy and Management

A. Policy responsibility and policy coherence

One overriding objective of Denmark's development co-operation is to achieve policy coherence in the country's relations with aid recipients. This is clearly stated by the Strategy adopted in 1994: "Danish development policy encompasses all our relations with developing countries, economic and political as well as multilateral and bilateral. The official development assistance is a central instrument in the development policy." An important step towards attaining this objective was the integration, in 1991, of official and private development co-operation, foreign policy, trade and other commercial considerations under the responsibility of the MFA. The need for a stronger concentration of political responsibilities had been expressed by Parliament in 1990, when its Commission on Foreign Relations presented a proposal to merge DANIDA and its functions with the Foreign Ministry in order to enhance policy coherence.

The reorganisation of the MFA resulted in the creation of two large services in the Ministry, the North Group and the South Group. The former has responsibility for relations with industrialised countries, Central and Eastern Europe and most states of the former Soviet Union. The South Group is responsible for relations in all policy areas with developing countries. Multilateral organisations are under the purview of either the North or the South Group, according to the main orientation of their activities. The new administrative structure of the MFA distributes responsibilities along geographical lines, as opposed to the earlier functional approach. The South Group is thus composed of departments for major regions, groupings of multilateral agencies and for special functions such as evaluation and research. Special units have been set up for environment and sustainable development, economic development analysis, mixed credits and gender affairs. A Technical Advisory Service, which had existed before the reorganisation of the Ministry, has been maintained. Given the generalist approach prevailing elsewhere in the South Group as a result of the restructuring, this Service has gained in importance based on its expertise in specific areas, such as tropical agriculture and medicine, environment, forestry, engineering, and macroeconomics. Since the reorganisation has brought about a wider sphere of activities for the South Group, some 30 officials have been transferred to it from other parts of the Ministry. Out of a total MFA staff of 1 400 persons, including embassy staff, close to 400 are now working in the South Group, including 119 officials with assignments abroad. Embassies have been set up in 19 major recipient countries of Danish bilateral ODA. Most of their staff have long-standing experience in development co-operation, especially those who had earlier served with DANIDA. The capacity to manage rapidly increasing bilateral ODA funds has been met through a corresponding increase in staff resources, an increase which has, in fact, been even brisker than that of the bilateral ODA volume. The number of staff per $10 million has been increased approximately from 4

Table 1. **Personnel stationed at headquarters and field offices**

	1989	1990	1991 [a]	1992	1993	1994
Number of staff members:						
Headquarters	203	208	198	238	259	275
Field offices	49	49	74	104	104	119
Total	**252**	**257**	**272**	**342**	**363**	**394**
For reference:						
Ratio Headquarter/ Field office staff	4.1	4.2	2.7	2.3	2.5	2.3

a) South Group, after reorganisation of MFA.
Source: DANIDA.

to 5 (see Table 1). This flexible staff policy has enabled Denmark to implement more complex and participatory approaches to aid management in the field.

The effects, and probably far-reaching consequences, of reform of the foreign service are difficult to assess fully even after four years. On the one hand, the reform has reduced the difficulties of co-ordinating the activities of different administrations and has thereby strengthened the potential for policy coherence. In addition, a clearer view of overall Danish relations with developing countries seems to have resulted from the reform. On the other hand, the efficiency gains achieved through bringing various policy areas under the responsibility of one administrative unit may have reduced the depth of professional expertise, the capacity to apply lessons learned and the institutional memory of the aid administration. Moreover, development concerns of a given aid recipient may, under these conditions, be mixed with conflicting national Danish interests. The appointment of a Minister for Development Co-operation in the MFA in 1993, two years after the reform, seems to indicate that strong political guidance is required to maintain the strong bias in favour of development co-operation in the MFA policy that earlier had characterised DANIDA's attitude and action.

Chart 1. **Ministry of Foreign Affairs**

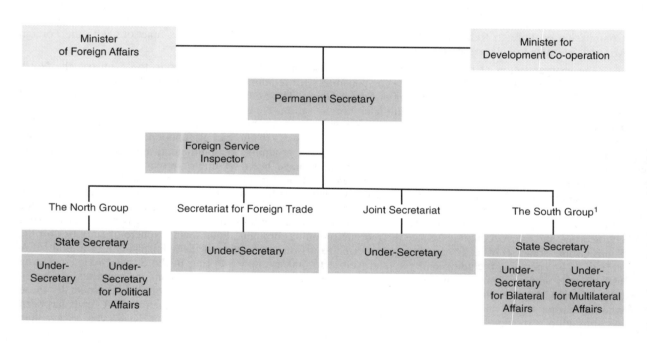

1. For detail see Chart 2.

B. Country programming, priority themes and special areas of bilateral co-operation

Country programming

Denmark programmes its bilateral assistance in advance, essentially concerning co-operation with a varying number of programme countries. The 1989 Plan of Action introduced systematic country programming, resulting in the formulation of country strategies. In addition to regular bilateral ODA, this procedure covered co-operation

Chart 2. **The South Group**

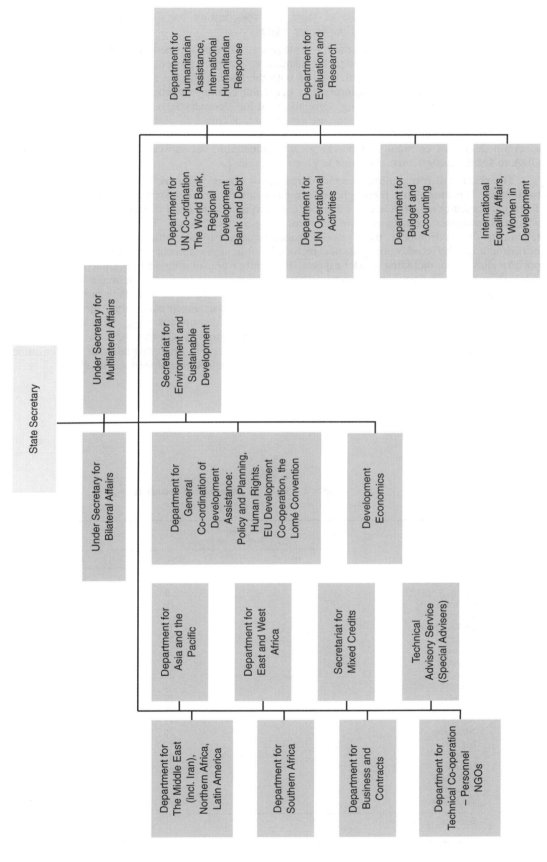

through Danish NGOs in the case of large and long-lasting engagements, in particular under framework agreements between DANIDA and the larger NGOs.

The 1994 Strategy maintains country strategies as a device for medium-term planning of bilateral assistance to the 20 Danish programme countries. New and more complex procedures for the formulation of strategies now ensure the participation of representatives of both the Danish and the recipient society in this process. Country strategies do not allocate ODA volumes to a particular country or programme. This function is fulfilled by the annual budget and the corresponding negotiations of the "country frame" between the Danish and the recipient governments. Annual ODA allocations are set out in a rolling five-year plan for the Danish aid programme and submitted to Parliament in December of each year. Although the figures of the plan are revised annually, it allows a certain degree of continuity in planning ODA allocations for individual recipients. The volume of bilateral ODA to Danish programme countries is given in Table 2.

The process of formulating a country strategy for one of Denmark's programme countries can be illustrated by that of Tanzania. This thorough and time-consuming process started in autumn 1994 when a group of Tanzanian researchers, NGOs and other bodies were invited to draft discussion papers on sectors which might benefit from Danish assistance, and on some cross-sectoral issues. The sectors included agriculture and its relation to the environment, water, health, general and vocational education, the private sector, and economic infrastructure. The cross-cutting issues included public management and accountability, human rights, and poverty alleviation, including gender aspects. The drafts were submitted to the Danish Embassy, who organised a seminar in Dar-es-Salaam in mid-April 1995 to discuss the papers and to make proposals for sectors to be retained in the country strategy. The results of the seminar in Tanzania were then discussed at another seminar in Denmark, with the participation of the Danish resource base. From early May, the South Group of the MFA, represented by the Southern Africa Department, started discussions with the Tanzanian authorities on the selection of sectors and forms of Danish aid for the future strategy. On this basis, the Embassy in Dar-es-Salaam has been asked to provide a first draft for the country strategy to be discussed with the Tanzanian authorities at the annual aid consultations scheduled for August 1995, before the Strategy is finalised.

Table 2. **ODA to programme countries**

$ million

	Net disbursements Two-year averages		Commitments 1993
	1987/88	1992/93	
Bangladesh	31	33	47
Benin	0	3	5
Bhutan	1	9	17
Bolivia	2	5	6
Burkina Faso	1	14	49
Egypt	21	25	18
Eritrea	–	0	–
Ghana	5	10	59
India	38	29	23
Ethiopia	3	12	1
Kenya	31	19	10
Mozambique	15	29	28
Nepal	9	13	10
Nicaragua	11	20	43
Niger	7	12	6
Tanzania	63	88	13
Uganda	8	41	18
Viet Nam	–	5	3
Zambia	6	17	17
Zimbabwe	10	27	6

Sign used: – Nil.

Priority themes

The Strategy sets out to strengthen Denmark's aid efforts in three thematic priority areas: population, trade and debt relief.

Population

In its bilateral programme Denmark has contributed only indirectly to the area of **population** through contributions to sectors with an impact on population growth. As a question of principle, there has been reluctance to launch direct population programmes.

For bilateral support to population activities, the Strategy contains a new, comprehensive concept entitled Sexual and Reproductive Health and Rights (SRHR). It deals with population issues within a broader health perspective and covers new target groups such as adolescents and men, as well as new topics such as infertility and sexually transmitted diseases. Family planning and Mother and Child Health Care are redefined as a component of SRHR.

This fresh approach to the population sector reflects the higher priority the Danish authorities now attach to this issue. In the preparatory process, Danish NGOs active in the population field have been given an opportunity to present viewpoints and ideas. The new population strategy is based on a concept which includes, but goes beyond, family planning. In general terms, the population strategy aims at strengthening the right of women and individual couples to determine the size of their families. Furthermore, guidelines for Danish bilateral and multilateral aid in the population field have been formulated. This concept also focuses on the environmental effects of population growth, such as environmental pressures created through migration from rural to urban areas. Pointing to the strong correlation between declining birth rates and progress in the social and economic sectors, the concept emphasizes that successful population programmes must be based on poverty alleviation and the improvement of women's and young girls' access to education, and to reproductive, and sexual health services.

Trade with developing countries

The Strategy's emphasis on improved foreign trade relations highlights the fact that Denmark's trade with developing countries must be considered modest compared to the performance of other DAC countries. A two-year average for 1992/93 shows that only some 9.5 per cent of Denmark's world trade – regardless of whether imports or exports are considered – takes place with developing countries, a share that has remained virtually unchanged in the five-year period starting in 1987/88. Still, Danish trade with developing countries has increased considerably in real terms over the five-year period 1987/88-1992/93, imports by over 3 per cent annually, exports by over 9 per cent. These ratios follow closely growth rates for total Danish trade, with exports to developing countries having grown somewhat faster than Danish world exports. Asia has been the most important region both with regard to imports and exports with an average real growth of Danish imports of 8 per cent per year between 1987/88 and 1992/93 (*cf.* Table 3 and Graph 1).

Denmark's largest trading partners were China, with 1.8 per cent of Danish world imports in 1992/93, Chinese Taipei with 0.8 per cent and South Korea with 0.6 per cent respectively. In all three cases manufactured goods have been the most important commodity group, particularly garments and footwear in the case of China. Central and South America is the second largest region with regard to developing country imports, accounting for 2 per cent of Danish world trade. Imports from Sub-Saharan Africa, the region where most Danish programme countries are located, showed a yearly increase of 4 per cent on average. As far as such programme countries are concerned, limited imports of agricultural goods came from Kenya, Mozambique, Tanzania, and Zimbabwe (not exceeding $5 million annually for each country). Sub-Saharan Africa can be expected to gain further importance in Danish imports, but starting from an admittedly very low level.

The bulk of Danish developing country exports is directed towards Asia (close to 4 per cent of Denmark's world trade), with South Korea receiving a significant and growing volume (there was a real annual growth of almost 9 per cent in the period 1987/88-1992/93); the dominating commodity group here has been manufactured goods, including a considerable share of garments and footwear. The second region in importance for Danish exports is North Africa and the Middle East (2.7 per cent of Danish world trade). Iran and Saudi Arabia are the region's main importers of Danish goods, principally manufactures.

The Strategy stresses, among other things, the importance of trade with developing countries and the need for support of such trade. Yet it appears that this policy has not yet been translated into action. DIPO, responsible for the promotion of imports from developing countries, received $0.54 million in 1994, the same as the previous year. DIPO is now initiating more extensive co-operation with five developing countries. The increase in imports

Table 3. Trade with developing countries

Imports

Imports	Constant 1991 $ million 1987/88	Constant 1991 $ million 1992/93	Av. annual growth 1987/88-1992/93	Percentages Share in world trade 1987/88	Percentages Share in world trade 1992/93
Sub-Saharan Africa	**88**	**109**	**4.2**	**0.3**	**0.4**
of which: South Africa	–	48	n.a.	–	0.2
North-Africa and Middle East	**491**	**151**	**–21.0**	**1.8**	**0.5**
of which: Israel	45	46	0.6	0.2	0.2
Asia	**1 280**	**1 857**	**7.7**	**4.7**	**6.2**
of which: Bangladesh	4	27	48.6	0.0	0.1
China	285	535	13.4	1.1	1.8
Chinese Taipei	197	243	4.3	0.7	0.8
Hong Kong	186	151	–4.1	0.7	0.5
India	65	99	8.8	0.2	0.3
Indonesia	56	135	19.1	0.2	0.5
Korea	189	188	–0.2	0.7	0.6
Malaysia	62	100	10.1	0.2	0.3
Pakistan	38	42	2.1	0.1	0.1
Philippines	27	30	2.4	0.1	0.1
Singapore	40	128	26.2	0.1	0.4
Thailand	91	125	6.4	0.3	0.4
America	**432**	**602**	**6.9**	**1.6**	**2.0**
of which: Argentina	122	170	6.9	0.5	0.6
Bahamas	1	37	103.5	0.0	0.1
Brazil	187	193	0.6	0.7	0.6
Colombia	32	98	25.0	0.1	0.3
Europe	**129**	**120**	**–1.4**	**0.5**	**0.4**
of which: Sts of Ex-Yugoslavia	66	31	–13.7	0.2	0.1
Turkey	50	81	10.2	0.2	0.3
Total bilateral allocable	**2 424**	**2 841**	**3.2**	**9.0**	**9.5**
Memo items:					
– Least developed countries	45	63	6.8	0.2	0.2
– Other low-income countries	496	866	11.8	1.8	2.9
– Lower middle-income countries	454	593	5.5	1.7	2.0
– Upper middle-income countries	640	702	1.9	2.4	2.4
– High-income countries	789	617	–4.8	2.9	2.1
– Unallocated (additional to total shown)	967	413	–15.6	3.6	1.4
World	**26 949**	**29 783**	**2.0**	**100.0**	**100.0**

Exports

Exports	Constant 1991 $ million 1987/88	Constant 1991 $ million 1992/93	Av. annual growth 1987/88-1992/93	Percentages Share in world trade 1987/88	Percentages Share in world trade 1992/93
Sub-Saharan Africa	**237**	**247**	**0.8**	**0.9**	**0.7**
North-Africa and Middle East	**712**	**996**	**7.0**	**2.7**	**2.9**
of which: Egypt	82	103	4.5	0.3	0.3
Iran	86	159	13.0	0.3	0.5
Israel	44	110	20.4	0.2	0.3
Kuwait	46	47	0.8	0.2	0.1
Saudi Arabia	155	238	9.0	0.6	0.7
United Arab Emirates	57	98	11.5	0.2	0.3
Asia	**791**	**1 269**	**9.9**	**3.0**	**3.7**
of which: China	115	56	–13.3	0.4	0.2
Chinese Taipei	77	128	10.8	0.3	0.2
Hong Kong	157	217	6.6	0.6	0.4
India	54	80	8.1	0.2	0.2
Indonesia	19	82	34.3	0.1	0.2
Korea	131	197	8.6	0.5	0.6
Malaysia	33	67	15.4	0.1	0.2
Singapore	75	113	8.7	0.3	0.3
Thailand	48	148	25.1	0.2	0.4
America	**229**	**532**	**18.3**	**0.9**	**1.6**
of which: Bahamas	4	102	89.6	0.0	0.3
Brazil	29	64	17.4	0.1	0.2
Mexico	25	102	32.2	0.1	0.3
Europe	**141**	**268**	**13.7**	**0.5**	**0.8**
of which: States of Ex-Yugoslavia	59	89	8.6	0.2	0.3
Turkey	46	109	18.7	0.2	0.3
Total bilateral allocable	**2 118**	**3 324**	**9.4**	**8.1**	**9.7**
Memo items:					
– Least developed countries	220	199	–2.0	0.8	0.6
– Other low-income countries	358	471	5.6	1.4	1.4
– Lower middle-income countries	488	910	13.3	1.9	2.7
– Upper middle-income countries	547	865	9.6	2.1	2.5
– High-income countries	504	877	11.7	1.9	2.6
– Unallocated (additional to total shown)	1 277	1 421	2.2	4.9	4.1
World	**26 074**	**34 291**	**5.6**	**100.0**	**100.0**

Signs used: – Nil.
n.a. Not applicable.
Note: Statistics exclude ships and off-shore oil platforms with exception of 1993, for which no such data have been reported. Countries selected on the basis of 1992/93 trade volume.

Graph 1. **Trade with developing countries**
US$ million at constant 1991 prices

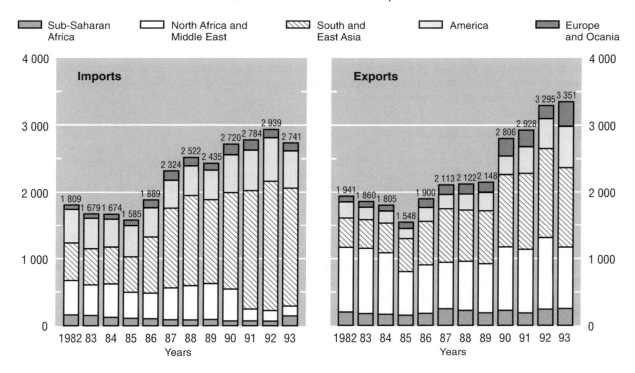

Sub-Saharan Africa | North Africa and Middle East | South and East Asia | America | Europe and Ocania

of $9 million over one year as a result of this co-operation is too limited, however, to have a noticeable impact on Denmark's overall trade with developing countries. The imports from developing countries are hampered by other political measures, however, such as the protection of Danish industry. The crisis in the Danish garment industry is often blamed on Third-World imports. In actual fact, only 34 per cent of Denmark's imports of textiles, garments and shoes emanate from developing countries, the most important share coming from countries in central and eastern Europe.

Debt relief

The first Danish debt forgiveness after the 1978 adoption of the United Nations Conference on Trade and Development (UNCTAD) resolution No. 165 (S-IX) on debt forgiveness took place in 1979. Between then and 1993, outstanding ODA debt of least developed countries (LLDCs) totalling DKr 2.5 billion, and of other low-income countries amounting to DKr 230 million, was cancelled.

Many of the 20 Danish programme countries are heavily indebted. The identified debt/GNP ratio of this group of countries (including Ethiopia) was 50 per cent in 1992, with the highest ratio for Nicaragua, whose total identified debt was five-and-a-half times greater than its GNP. Mozambique with a debt/GNP ratio of 478 per cent was second on the list of highly indebted programme countries, followed by Tanzania and Zambia.

The programme countries' debt to multilateral organisations, concessional and non-concessional taken together, is in some cases considerable. In 1992 the average multilateral debt/GNP ratio for the group of programme countries as a whole equalled 13 per cent, but in cases such as Mozambique, Tanzania, and Zambia this ratio exceeded 80 per cent. Since the rules of international financial institutions, to which this debt is owed, do not allow debt forgiveness, this serious situation offers a possibility for Denmark to initiate debt relief in this area. So far, such actions have been undertaken, on a modest scale, in 1990 and 1992 with Danish contributions to the Support Group for Zambia and to the settlement of Nicaragua's arrears to the IMF and the World Bank. Denmark also contributed to the settlement of Uganda's arrears to the East African and African Development Banks. The Strategy promises stronger Danish efforts in this field. In addition to active participation in multilateral debt relief arrangements, these efforts will include bilateral contributions towards interest payments and reimbursements to multilateral institutions, of which Denmark is a member.

In 1995, Denmark revised its policy with regard to forgiveness of ODA debt. The new criteria for eligibility are: LLDC-status; Low-income and "highly indebted" status, both according to World Bank criteria; and status as one of Denmark's programme co-operation countries. Priority will be given to countries that meet several of these criteria. These objective criteria can be modified by a case-by-case evaluation, in particular with regard to each country's record in the field of human rights and political will to implement economic reforms. The first application of these criteria could result in the cancellation of approximately DKr 1 billion of ODA-debt, representing about one sixth of outstanding ODA-loans.

Special areas of bilateral co-operation

The Strategy stipulates that apart from co-operation with the programme countries, bilateral co-operation will be confined to special areas, especially human rights and democratisation, associated financing and transitional assistance. Under certain conditions, programme countries can also benefit from these forms of aid, in addition to co-operation with Danish NGOs.

Human rights and democratisation

The promotion of the respect for human rights, and the concept of "good government" play an increasingly important role in the Danish aid programme. Denmark has taken a clear position concerning the fostering of democratisation and human rights, taking into account individual countries' performance in this respect (*e.g.* reduction of ODA to Kenya, stepping-up of ODA to Nepal and reconsideration of development aid to Ethiopia).

Associated financing

Despite its name, the Danish Mixed Credit programme of 1993 is not a typical associated financing or mixed credit scheme, since there are not two combined financial transactions (ODA and a commercial credit), but only one export credit, the interest rate of which is reduced by a subsidy granted from the aid budget (concessionality element 50 per cent for least developed, 35 per cent for other recipient countries). This is the solution also chosen by Sweden for its "concessionary credits", under which only the subsidy amount is reported as ODA. The Danish scheme has as yet not recorded any disbursements of subsidies, for which a DKr 300 million ($47 million) line was allocated in the 1994 budget. A large number of Danish export credits for developing countries are presently being processed – 40 per cent of which for China – by a special Secretariat in the South Group of the Ministry of Foreign Affairs (see Box 2).

Transitional assistance

This type of assistance will be awarded to create or recreate preconditions for economic and social development in countries which are undergoing basic social restructuring, usually in connection with the termination of armed conflict or transition from a centrally controlled economy to a market-based economic system. Transitional assistance will be awarded for a limited period and will be used selectively. Assistance will

---

Box 2.   Mixed Credit Programme in the Philippines

At the beginning of 1995, the Committee for Mixed Credits (CMC) granted interest subsidies totalling $8.2 million for a $25 million credit line for the Philippines. The Danish Export Finance Corporation (DEF) will be the creditor, and the loan agreement should have been concluded with the Development Bank of the Philippines (DBP) in the first half of 1995.

The credit line was established with the DBP in order to finance small Danish supplies of under $4 million to the Philippines for small-scale investments in the manufacturing sector in less developed regions, environment investments and investments in water supply and infrastructure in rural areas. The credit procedure requires the request by a local buyer that the DBP should fund Danish supplies. If the DBP agrees with the request, it will ask DEF to finance the delivery through the credit line.

predominantly comprise product supply, assistance to multilateral programmes or programmes implemented by non-governmental organisations.

Private sector development programme

This new programme, initiated in 1993, is supposed to serve two objectives, through the establishment of long-term contacts between Danish and recipient country industry: first, to help local enterprises in acquiring technology and know-how; second, to reduce the risk for Danish enterprises in joint ventures, an objective which is also pursued by IFU. Another Danish institution, DIPO, ensures that relations between Danish industry and developing countries are not one-way, but develop in both directions. The rationale of these objectives is that they would help Danish industry to develop markets in developing countries. This rationale is related to the political target of 50 per cent return on Danish aid: Danish enterprises may be in a better position to win aid-financed contracts if they are in close and long-term relationship with the recipient country and with enterprises there who might be beneficiaries of Danish aid. There are currently 70 co-operation projects waiting to be processed and supported by the aid administration. The Private Sector Development Programme is a pilot programme, limited at the moment to Ghana, India and Zimbabwe. The programme will be reviewed in 1995 to determine necessary changes.

C. Decentralisation of aid management

Although the restructuring of the MFA, in particular its merger with DANIDA, could be regarded as a move towards concentration of responsibilities, the aid authorities have continued to decentralise the tasks related to the management of the aid programme.

Embassies assist the recipient country authorities in identifying and planning new activities and in monitoring projects funded through the Danish aid programme. With the declared purpose of maximising cost effectiveness and further enhancing the quality of ODA, the MFA is currently examining the possibility of further decentralising decision-making authority from headquarters to the field. This process was initiated in 1988, when embassies were authorised to approve minor projects and enter into contracts with, for example, indigenous private enterprises, local NGOs, etc. up to a maximum amount of DKr 1 million ($0.15 million). The amount was increased to DKr 3 million ($0.5 million) in 1992. In 1994 a study was carried out to assess the effectiveness of the Local Grant Authority for Danish Embassies. The conclusions of the study, which were positive in the main, welcomed the fact that requests for support could be rapidly met through the Local Grant Authority. Among negative aspects, however, the evaluation mentioned inadequate economic and financial sustainability of projects financed, in some instances a lack of knowledge of the objectives of Danish development aid, and insufficient experience of project officers in successfully conducting the project cycle. On the basis of this assessment the MFA has revised its instructions regarding the Local Grant Authority with effect from 1 January 1995.

The strength of the decentralisation process is borne out by a corresponding increase in staff numbers at the embassies. While there has been a substantial increase of staff at the South Group's headquarters, administrative personnel in the field has grown even more rapidly, as indicated clearly in the ratio headquarters/field office staff, which has fell from 4.1 to 2.3 between 1989 and 1994.

Local ownership of development

In formulating strategies for programme countries aid management now includes a strong element of participation and ownership by the societies in programme countries. Groups of local academics and NGOs are asked to prepare discussion papers on the needs in certain areas or sectors which Denmark could be expected to satisfy. These findings are the subject of seminars in the respective programme countries in which representatives of the recipient government, local NGOs and Parliamentarians participate. The papers, and the discussion during the seminars, should also cover the role of aid programmes of other donors in the country concerned. Only after these seminars have defined issues of high priority, the country desk in the MFA develops a draft for a country- and sector-strategy for discussion with the Danish resource base.

Another move towards local ownership is evident in the intention expressed in the Strategy to increase the use of local technical advisors in Danish supported programmes. This initiative contributes to developing local capacity for programme implementation. Local participation in the assessment of results, *e.g.* through evaluation, also needs to be strengthened. Improved local management capacity, especially in the area of financial administration and control, would automatically improve local capacity for evaluation.

The move in Danish bilateral assistance towards sector programmes and support for decentralised public sector activities in its programme countries requires increased participation of middle- and lower-level local administrations in preparing and implementing development programmes. Denmark has therefore begun to provide technical and financial assistance to a number of its programme countries to improve public sector capacity, (*e.g.* Nepal, Nicaragua, and Uganda), to enable them to undertake these tasks.

In the specific area of aid management and accountability Denmark has supported the UNDDSMS in the development of a "Framework for Harmonized Aid Management and Accountability" which contains basic elements of aid management and accountability. It also represents a foundation for co-operation between the donor community and developing countries in support of the latter's ultimate responsibility for formulating and managing their development processes and being held responsible for results.

In this context, Denmark is currently supporting the management of the recurrent and development budget of the health sector in Zambia. Assistance for capacity building of public administrations will be a component of future Danish aid programmes, to enable national administrations in programme countries to exercise fully their responsibility for planning, budgeting, accounting and auditing. At the same time, the Danish initiative can further the objective of reducing and harmonizing donor's accounting requirements, thereby alleviating the administrative burden of recipient countries for aid management. However, better donor co-ordination at recipient country level would be required to achieve this objective.

D. Assessment of results

DANIDA's Evaluation Unit, which was created in 1982, was strengthened and made more independent from aid management in 1991 when the aid administration was restructured and the South Group created. The Unit still has only four staff members and contracts out all studies to external consultancies, with the occasional participation of an official from the South Group. The Evaluation Unit prepares an annual plan of evaluations, negotiates the terms of reference of the studies and monitors ongoing evaluation work.

Initially evaluations were essentially used to assess the efficiency of project management, but a gradual shift seems to be taking place in the direction of more general studies of themes and sectors of aid. General country studies are not yet part of the Unit's activities but the Danish authorities consider that in future greater priority may have to be given to assessing the wider impact of the aid activities concerned on the recipients' development process.

The involvement of recipient country authorities in the evaluation process has so far been limited. The authorities of these countries are invited to comment on relevant studies in draft form, but not many use this opportunity to participate in the assessment of aid. Recipient partner countries normally agree to the release of evaluation results. Subsequently, a full report is published in Denmark. Occasionally, negotiations of the text to be published are required if conclusions of the study are felt to be unsubstantiated. Nevertheless the authors of the study have the final say about its content.

Feedback of evaluation findings takes place mainly at two levels: discussions of the draft reports with operational personnel, and information transmitted to decision-makers within the Ministry. This feedback procedure has a rather informal character.

A major evaluation study on Danish BoP support was published in 1994. The study covered five out of twelve developing countries which together had received some $300 million of Danish ODA as BoP support. The study focused on three aspects: the role of BoP support in structural adjustment, as a form of bilateral aid, and as an aid policy instrument, and resulted in the following findings:

i) BoP support can help structural adjustment by filling the national savings gap which is constraining growth. To be useful, however, it should no longer be provided in the form of commodity import support, but take the form of untied budget support, since demand for foreign exchange is shrinking during the process of structural adjustment.

ii) BoP support, in its usual form of tied import financing, appeared not to be a form of effective aid. The costs of Danish commodities financed by tied import support are higher than those of imports financed under international competitive bidding. Also, DANIDA allegedly did not pay enough attention to the ways in which local counterpart funds resulting from BoP support were administered. Monitoring of these funds was inadequate and DANIDA tacitly accepted that parastatals paid only part of the value of commodities they had received.

iii) Denmark's use of BoP support as an aid policy instrument in the dialogue with recipients did not increase the recipients' motivation to undertake structural adjustment.

Denmark participates actively in the work of the DAC Expert Group on Aid Evaluation, and in this context has initiated a study on donor experience supporting developing countries' capacity for evaluation. This study is part of the Group's evaluation of assistance for public sector management. Denmark also participates in a number of joint evaluations. In 1994 it assumed overall co-ordinating responsibility for a joint evaluation of emergency aid to Rwanda. Sweden, Norway, the United Kingdom and the United States conduct studies on specific aspects of this theme. Denmark also participated in another joint evaluation exercise in 1994 which assessed regional development banks.

In 1994, the MFA put in place a scheme for monitoring the effectiveness of international aid agencies. The rationale for this exercise was to provide the basis for informed decisions on Denmark's participation in the activities of such agencies given the new concept of "active multilateralism". The main objective of monitoring multilateral effectiveness is to determine the extent to which international aid agencies effectively use their comparative advantages within the overall framework of assistance to developing countries, both among them-selves and in relation to bilateral donor agencies. The monitoring focuses on typical strengths and weaknesses of the agencies and not on the success or failure of individual projects and programmes. The monitoring exercise also provides the basis for a deepened policy dialogue between Denmark and the international agencies.

Each year, the monitoring system selects one multilateral agency from each of the three groups of multilat-eral agencies, the UN programmes proper, the UN specialised agencies and the development banks and funds. In 1994, the Food and Agriculture Organisation of the United Nations (FAO), United Nations Fund for Popula-tion (UNFPA) and African Development Bank (AfDB) were selected, and in 1995, UNDP, UNESCO and the Asian Development Bank (AsDB) were included in the monitoring exercise. The monitoring, which is essentially performed by Danish Embassies, takes place both at headquarters of agencies and at field level. Field level monitoring primarily concerns the capacity of the agencies to design and implement activities. Developing countries selected for this exercise are Bangladesh, Ghana, India, Kenya, Mozambique, Nicaragua, Tanzania, Uganda, Zimbabwe, all of which are Danish programme countries.

Chapter III

Aid Volume Trends, Conditions and Focus of Bilateral Assistance

A. Trends and composition of financial flows

The target set by Parliament in 1985 to reach an ODA volume of 1 per cent of GNP by 1992 was attained according to schedule. The ODA/GNP ratio in 1992 was 1.02 per cent and the intention is to maintain it around the 1 per cent level. Graph 2 shows the development of Denmark's ODA volume in terms of GNP during the last decade. Danish ODA performance has been facilitated through a revolving five-year planning procedure with expenditure frames submitted once a year to Parliament by the Government. Following the United Nations Conference on Environment and Development (UNCED), in December 1992 Parliament decided to establish an Environment and Disaster Relief Fund. Appropriations for this Fund, which are additional to the ODA budget, should attain 0.5 per cent of GNP by 2002. In 1995, DKr 1.4 billion ($0.2 billion) was committed for measures to be financed from the Fund, half of which for refugees living in Denmark, the rest for actions in the field of environment in both Eastern Europe and developing countries.

With an ODA volume of $1.3 billion in 1993, corresponding to 1.03 per cent of GNP, Denmark ranked first among DAC Member countries in relative terms. Compared to 1992, ODA increased by 2 per cent at constant prices, due to a 5 per cent rise in the bilateral programme, while multilateral contributions declined by 3 per cent (see Table 4). A trend of continuing economic growth can be perceived in Denmark, with an average annual

Graph 2. **ODA net disbursements, 1982-93**

At constant 1992 prices and as a share of GNP

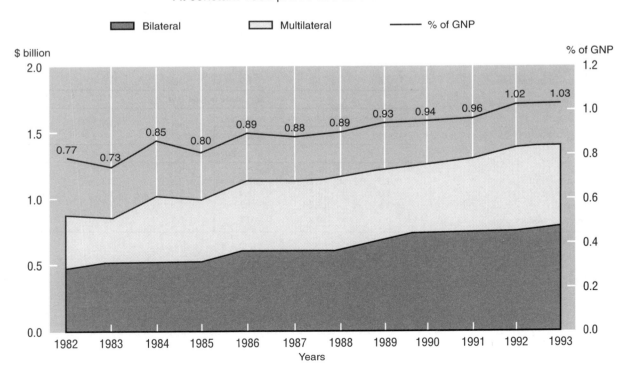

Table 4. **Main ODA volume indicators**

	i) Disbursements and commitments					
	Two-year averages over ten-year period			1991	1992	1993
	1982/83	1987/88	1992/93			
ODA net disbursements						
Current prices and exchange rates						
($ million)	405	891	1 366	1 200	1 392	1 340
Bilateral	226	468	755	686	756	755
Multilateral	179	422	610	514	635	585
1992 prices and exchange rates						
($ million)	846	1 136	1 403	1 296	1 392	1 414
Bilateral	472	598	776	741	756	796
Multilateral	374	538	627	555	635	618
National currency (DKr million)	3 535	6 041	8 544	7 678	8 403	8 685
Bilateral	1 977	3 178	4 729	4 391	4 567	4 891
Multilateral	1 558	2 863	3 815	3 288	3 836	3 795
GNP ratios (%)	0.75	0.88	1.03	0.96	1.02	1.03
Bilateral	0.42	0.46	0.57	0.55	0.56	0.58
Multilateral	0.33	0.42	0.46	0.41	0.47	0.45
ODA commitments						
Current prices and exchange rates						
($ million)	454	899	1 516	1 111	1 424	1 608
Bilateral	271	529	900	657	798	1 002
Multilateral	183	370	616	453	626	606
GNP ratios (%)	0.84	0.89	1.14	0.89	1.05	1.24
Bilateral	0.50	0.52	0.68	0.53	0.59	0.77
Multilateral	0.34	0.37	0.46	0.36	0.46	0.47

	ii) Average annual growth rates of ODA disbursements in real terms					
	1982/83-1992/93	1987/88-1992/93	1982/83-1992/93	For reference: Total DAC		
				1982/83-1987/88	1987/88-1992/93	1982/83-1992/93
	Percentages					
Total ODA	6.1	4.3	5.2	2.5	1.6	2.1
Bilateral	4.8	5.4	5.1	3.6	1.3	2.4
Multilateral	7.5	3.1	5.3	0.5	2.1	1.3
For reference:						
GNP growth in real terms	2.6	1.2	1.9	3.6	2.6	3.1

	iii) Share in total DAC					
	Two-year averages over ten-year period			1991	1992	1993
	1982/83	1987/88	1992/93			
	Percentages					
Total ODA	1.5	2.0	2.3	2.1	2.3	2.4
Bilateral	1.3	1.5	1.9	1.7	1.8	1.9
Multilateral	1.9	3.2	3.3	3.3	3.2	3.4
Gross national product	0.7	0.8	0.7	0.7	0.7	0.7

Note: Details may not add up to totals because of rounding.

increase of GNP in real terms of 3 per cent projected for the period 1994-96. Given the official commitment to the 1 per cent of GNP target, a similar growth can therefore be expected for the Danish ODA volume. According to preliminary reporting, ODA disbursements in 1994 amounted to $1.5 billion, or 1.03 per cent of GNP, which corresponds to a growth rate of 2.5 per cent over the 1993 volume (see Table 5). Under the current five-year plan, ODA appropriations are expected to grow at the following rates (as a percentage compared to the previous year): 1995, 3.6; 1996, 4; 1997, 4.1; 1998, 3.5. While the central government budget has increased sharply over the last three years, ODA appropriations as a share of this budget have dropped, from 3.2 per cent in 1991 to 2.5 per cent in 1993, which is still the second largest ratio among DAC countries. This is the consequence of the decision not to increase the ODA volume after the attainment of the 1 per cent of GNP target.

Following two years of stagnation at $1 billion, total financial flows from Denmark to developing countries started to grow again in 1992 (see Table 6). However, non-ODA flows which have often been negative during the

Table 5. **ODA volume in 1994**

		Denmark		Total DAC	
		$ million	Real term change over previous year	$ million	Real term change over previous year
Bilateral		**801.8**	**0.6**	**40 156**	**−2.1**
Grants		823.5	1.4	35 065	0.9
Loans		−21.7	n.a.	5 091	−19.1
Multilateral		**648.4**	**4.9**	**17 590**	**−1.3**
of which:	UN agencies	304.6	8.7	4 013	−6.1
	EC	98.9	0.5	4 567	8.
	World Bank Group	82.0	−6.1	5 112	−9.7
	Regional development banks	60.3	82.4	2 650	0.7
Total ODA		**1 450.2**	**2.5**	**57 800**	**−1.8**
For reference:					
ODA/GNP ratio, *per cent*		1.03	−	0.29	−

Note: Based on preliminary reporting.

Table 6. **Total financial flows**

Net disbursements in $ million at current prices and exchange rates

	1982/83	1987/88	1991	1992	1993
ODA	**405**	**891**	**1 200**	**1 392**	**1 340**
Other official flows	**170**	**−111**	**24**	**−91**	**−12**
Official export credits	164	−101	53	−82	−
Equities and other bilateral assets	3	16	−7	−1	−1
Multilateral	4	−25	−21	−7	−11
Private non-concessional flows	**363**	**−11**	**−172**	**260**	**24**
Direct investment	27	74	9	121	101
Bilateral portfolio investment	−	−	−	−	−
Multilateral portfolio investment	79	−	−	−	−
Private export credits	257	−85	−181	139	−77
Private grants	**11**	**22**	**28**	**45**	**45**
Total non-ODA flows	**545**	**−100**	**−120**	**214**	**57**
As share of GNP (%)	1.01	−0.10	−0.10	0.16	0.04
Total flows	**950**	**790**	**1 080**	**1 605**	**1 397**
As share of GNP (%)	1.75	0.79	0.87	1.18	1.08

Sign used: − Nil.

late 1980s and the early 1990s, represented only 13 per cent and 4 per cent of total flows in 1992 and 1993, respectively.

In 1993, $755 million were disbursed as bilateral ODA and contributions to international aid agencies amounted to $585 million, resulting in a ratio of 56:44 between bilateral and multilateral ODA. In 1994, the ratio of bilateral to multilateral ODA was 55:45. In earlier years, the same ratio of distribution for total ODA flows prevailed, with only minor fluctuations (see Table 7). This is a relatively high share compared to the average of DAC Members' multilateral ODA, which fluctuated between 26 and 31 per cent in recent years. Main recipient institutions of Danish multilateral ODA in 1993 were UNDP (15 per cent of multilateral ODA), UNFPA (3 per cent), UNICEF (4 per cent), IDA (14 per cent), Regional Funds (5 per cent), and European programmes (16 per cent).

B. Regional and sectoral distribution of bilateral ODA

The Strategy document notes that ''In the weakest countries, the problem of poverty can only be resolved if the efforts of individual countries are supported by official development assistance from a range of donor countries. Denmark will participate in and contribute to this co-operation...»

Regional distribution

Denmark has traditionally concentrated assistance on poor developing countries, whose share regularly reached or surpassed 90 per cent of bilateral disbursements, compared to a DAC average of around 60 per cent (see Table 8). While there is no reason to doubt that this concentration of Danish aid also prevailed in 1992 and 1993, the large amount of unallocated disbursements – one-third of the total – to particular recipient countries does not allow further analysis of these data. A certain shift in the geographical distribution of ODA in the direction of relatively wealthier developing countries may be expected, however, when the recently introduced Mixed Credit Programme gains momentum. These countries are more likely to fulfil the condition of creditworthiness required under the Programme. The Sub-Saharan region in Africa has been and is benefiting the most from Danish ODA with a share of over 60 per cent. The share for Asia has dropped somewhat recently (*e.g.* for China and Bangladesh), while the amount disbursed for American developing countries (in particular Nicaragua) increased modestly.

In 1992/93, 90 developing countries received assistance from Denmark in one form or the other. Five years earlier, the number of recipients was 76 (see Table 9). However, the bulk of bilateral ODA – 84 per cent in 1992/93 – is spent on only 20 countries. Among these, figure 16 of Denmark's programme countries, the four others – Benin, Bolivia, Eritrea and Viet Nam – having received only minor sums or no aid at all during this two-year period. Regular development assistance to four countries on the list of major recipients – China, Namibia, Thailand and Yemen – will be phased out by the year 2000, while aid for these countries in the so-called special areas will not be restricted.

Eligibility for the provision of bilateral ODA is restricted to an upper limit of $1 765 per capita (December 1993) for recipients of project assistance, consultancy assistance, NGO project assistance and volunteer aid. With regard to multi-bilateral assistance, scholarships and aid intended for particularly poor areas the income limit has been set at $2 500 per capita.

Since the majority of the Danish programme countries are situated in **Sub-Saharan Africa,** this region accounts for the largest share of bilateral allocable ODA. In 1993, 63 per cent of Danish allocable aid was channelled to Sub-Saharan African recipients, most of it to low-income countries. While such aid flows increased by more than 5 per cent annually in the five-year period 1982/83-1987/88, since then they have more or less levelled off and the average annual growth rate in the following five-year period was only 1 per cent. The most significant recipients of Danish ODA in this region have been Tanzania and Uganda. Although overall bilateral Danish ODA is only 2.4 per cent of the DAC total, Danish aid disbursed in 1993 to these two African recipients equalled 13 per cent of the aid they received from all DAC countries. Such figures reflect clearly the leverage Danish development co-operation might have in some of its programme countries. Examples of Danish assistance to Uganda are provided in Box 3.

Asia (excluding the Middle East) is the second most important recipient region for Danish co-operation. In 1993 ODA flows to this region amounted to 23 per cent of Danish allocable bilateral ODA. These ODA flows have shown a decline of over 3 per cent annually in the period 1987/88-1992/93. Major recipients in the region are Bangladesh and India, which received $30 million each in constant prices in 1993. Danish ODA to China fell by nearly 75 per cent from the previous year and amounted to a mere $4 million.

Table 7. **ODA net disbursements by main categories**

	At constant 1992 prices and exchange rates $ million				% of total net ODA				*For reference:* Total DAC: % of total net ODA			
	1987/88	1991	1992	1993	1987/88	1991	1992	1993	1987/88	1991	1992	1993
Bilateral	**598**	**741**	**756**	**796**	**52.6**	**57.2**	**54.4**	**56.3**	**69.4**	**73.7**	**68.7**	**69.6**
Grants	519	749	772	811	45.7	57.8	55.5	57.4	53.6	62.3	55.5	59.1
Development projects and programmes	332	447	407	471	29.2	34.5	29.3	33.3	20.3	17.3	15.2	15.0
Technical co-operation	102	145	162	172	8.9	11.2	11.6	12.2	20.6	21.0	21.7	23.2
Food aid	–	–	–	–	–	–	–	–	4.0	2.8	2.8	2.4
Emergency aid (other than food aid)	–	57	105	81	–	4.4	7.5	5.8	1.6	4.1	4.1	5.7
Debt forgiveness	45	7	21	5	3.9	0.5	1.5	0.4	0.5	10.3	4.8	4.8
Support through NGOs	8	4	4	7	0.7	0.3	0.3	0.5	1.7	1.9	1.6	1.9
Administrative costs	32	48	52	56	2.8	3.7	3.7	4.0	3.5	3.7	3.9	4.5
Other grants	1	40	21	18	0.1	3.1	1.5	1.2	1.2	1.3	1.3	1.6
Loans	78	–8	–15	–15	6.9	–0.6	–1.1	–1.1	15.9	11.3	13.3	10.5
For reference:												
Associated financing	–	–	–	–	–	–	–	–	1.0	0.7	1.0	0.9
Multilateral	**538**	**555**	**635**	**618**	**47.4**	**42.8**	**45.6**	**43.7**	**30.6**	**26.3**	**31.3**	**30.4**
UN agencies	254	262	289	280	22.4	20.2	20.7	19.8	7.4	7.5	7.5	7.2
of which: WFP	37	36	52	43	3.2	2.7	3.8	3.0	1.5	1.3	1.3	1.3
UNDP	93	90	91	94	8.2	6.9	6.6	6.6	2.0	1.8	1.7	1.6
UNICEF	14	29	31	30	1.3	2.2	2.2	2.1	0.7	0.6	0.7	0.6
UNFPA	14	17	19	21	1.2	1.3	1.4	1.5	0.4	0.4	0.4	0.4
EC	74	89	81	98	6.5	6.9	5.8	6.9	5.2	7.5	6.9	7.3
World Bank group	92	81	81	96	8.1	6.2	5.8	6.8	12.0	8.5	11.2	9.6
of which: IDA	81	81	79	87	7.2	6.2	5.7	6.1	10.9	8.0	10.0	8.9
Regional development banks	1	–	55	33	0.1	–	4.0	2.3	4.3	1.0	3.8	4.5
Other multilateral	117	123	129	111	10.3	9.5	9.3	7.9	1.7	1.9	1.8	1.8
Total ODA net disbursements	**1 136**	**1 296**	**1 392**	**1 414**	**100.0**	**100.0**	**100.0**	**100.0**	**100.0**	**100.0**	**100.0**	**100.0**
of which: Food aid	41	52	–	10	3.6	4.0	–	0.7	7.8	6.0	5.3	4.6

Sign used: – Nil.

Table 8. **Allocable ODA by major groupings, regions and main recipients**

Net disbursements

i) Summary table

	ODA disbursements at constant 1992 prices and exchange rates ($ million)				Average annual change in real terms		Share of bilateral ODA (Per cent)				For reference: Total DAC: share of bilateral ODA			
	1982/83	1987/88	1992	1993	1982/83-1987/88	1987/88-1992/93	1982/83	1987/88	1992	1993	1982/83	1987/88	1992	1993
Sub-Saharan Africa	**236**	**307**	**308**	**340**	**5.4**	**1.1**	**57.2**	**60.2**	**62.0**	**63.3**	**29.3**	**33.7**	**30.9**	**32.7**
Low-income countries	220	277	295	325	4.7	2.3	53.3	54.3	59.4	60.5	24.7	28.6	24.7	24.9
Other	16	30	13	15	13.2	-14.4	3.9	5.9	2.6	2.7	4.6	5.1	6.2	7.8
North Africa and Middle East	**17**	**39**	**30**	**36**	**17.8**	**-3.3**	**4.1**	**7.6**	**6.0**	**6.7**	**21.0**	**16.8**	**20.5**	**14.7**
Low-income countries	10	41	27	34	33.1	-5.4	2.3	8.0	5.5	6.4	8.8	6.7	8.9	6.1
Other	7	-2	3	1	n.a.	n.a.	1.8	-0.3	0.6	0.2	12.3	10.1	11.6	8.6
Asia	**151**	**146**	**124**	**121**	**-0.7**	**-3.4**	**36.5**	**28.7**	**25.0**	**22.6**	**28.7**	**30.3**	**29.9**	**30.6**
Low-income countries	144	136	108	111	-1.1	-4.3	34.8	26.8	21.8	20.7	23.6	24.3	22.7	23.6
Other	7	10	16	10	6.2	6.4	1.7	1.9	3.2	1.9	5.1	6.0	7.1	6.9
America	**9**	**18**	**35**	**40**	**16.3**	**15.4**	**2.1**	**3.6**	**7.0**	**7.4**	**12.0**	**12.5**	**11.1**	**12.2**
Low-income countries	2	15	18	24	49.5	7.1	0.5	2.9	3.7	4.4	1.8	2.1	2.2	1.9
Other	7	3	17	16	-12.6	37.1	1.6	0.7	3.4	3.0	10.3	10.4	8.8	10.4
Oceania	**0**	**–**	**–**	**0**	**-100.0**	**n.a.**	**0.0**	**–**	**–**	**0.0**	**6.0**	**4.9**	**3.6**	**4.4**
Europe	**0**	**-0**	**-0**	**0**	**n.a.**	**-10.3**	**0.0**	**-0.0**	**-0.1**	**0.0**	**3.0**	**1.8**	**4.1**	**5.5**
Total bilateral allocable	**413**	**510**	**496**	**537**	**4.3**	**0.3**	**100.0**	**100.0**	**100.0**	**100.0**	**100.0**	**100.0**	**100.0**	**100.0**
Memo items:														
Least developed countries	226	284	305	331	4.7	2.3	54.6	55.7	61.4	61.8	29.4	32.3	25.7	27.1
Other low-income countries	150	185	144	163	4.3	-3.7	36.3	36.3	29.0	30.4	29.9	29.8	33.2	29.8
Lower middle-income countries	35	25	45	40	-6.8	11.0	8.6	4.9	9.0	7.4	24.7	24.6	30.3	31.6
Upper middle-income countries	2	16	3	3	54.5	-29.3	0.4	3.2	0.6	0.5	6.1	5.2	3.2	5.0
High-income countries	–	-0	–	0	n.a.	NA	–	-0.1	–	0.0	9.8	8.0	7.7	6.5
Unallocated (additional to total shown)	59	88	260	260	8.4	24.2	14.2	17.3	52.5	48.4	16.9	22.5	22.5	23.6

Signs used: – Nil.

0 or 0.0: Less than half the smallest unit shown.

n.a.: Not applicable.

Table 8. Allocable ODA by major groupings, regions and main recipients (cont'd)

Net disbursements

ii) Detailed table

	1992 $ million				Denmark's ODA as a share of total DAC ODA (%)			
	1982/83	1987/88	1992	1993	1982/83	1987/88	1992	1993
Sub-Saharan Africa	**236**	**307**	**308**	**340**	**2.5**	**2.9**	**2.8**	**3.1**
Low-income countries	220	277	295	325	2.8	3.1	3.4	3.9
of which: Burkina Faso	4	1	8	21	1.5	0.4	2.8	7.8
Ethiopia	5	4	7	17	2.8	0.7	1.5	3.7
Ghana	-0	7	6	14	-0.2	3.0	1.8	4.3
Kenya	39	40	19	20	5.6	5.9	3.6	4.4
Mozambique	14	20	27	34	4.2	2.4	2.6	3.9
Niger	3	8	16	8	1.3	2.8	6.0	3.1
Sudan	18	11	5	3	2.1	1.8	2.6	1.9
Tanzania	84	81	95	85	8.8	8.4	11.6	12.5
Uganda	4	10	37	48	3.7	6.0	14.6	13.1
Zambia	10	7	18	16	2.6	1.6	2.5	3.0
Zimbabwe	10	13	26	29	3.0	4.1	4.9	8.9
North-Africa and Middle East	**17**	**39**	**30**	**36**	**0.3**	**0.7**	**0.4**	**0.7**
Low-income countries	10	41	27	34	0.4	1.9	0.9	1.7
of which: Egypt	7	27	23	28	0.3	1.4	0.8	1.5
Yemen	3	13	4	7	1.5	6.4	2.8	3.5
Asia	**151**	**146**	**124**	**121**	**1.7**	**1.5**	**1.2**	**1.2**
Low-income countries	144	136	108	111	1.9	1.8	1.4	1.4
of which: Bangladesh	47	39	37	30	3.2	3.3	4.4	4.3
China	14	27	15	4	1.4	2.1	0.7	0.2
India	70	49	30	30	5.5	4.0	2.5	3.4
Nepal	1	11	9	17	0.4	4.1	3.4	6.6
Lower middle-income countries	7	10	14	10	0.5	0.6	0.6	0.5
of which: Thailand	7	6	7	5	1.2	0.9	1.0	0.8
America	**9**	**18**	**35**	**40**	**0.2**	**0.5**	**0.9**	**1.0**
Low-income countries	2	15	18	24	0.4	2.2	2.3	3.9
of which: Nicaragua	2	14	18	23	1.2	7.6	3.7	8.3
Lower middle-income countries	6	3	18	16	0.3	0.1	0.7	0.7
Total bilateral allocable	**413**	**510**	**496**	**537**	**1.3**	**1.6**	**1.4**	**1.6**
Memo items:								
Least developed countries	226	284	305	331	2.4	2.8	3.3	3.6
Other low-income countries	150	185	144	163	1.6	2.0	1.2	1.7
Lower middle-income countries	35	25	45	40	0.4	0.3	0.4	0.4
Upper middle-income countries	2	16	3	3	0.1	1.0	0.3	0.2
High-income countries	–	-0	–	0	–	-0.0	–	0.0
Unallocated (additional to total shown)	59	88	260	260	1.1	1.2	3.3	3.3

Signs used: – Nil.
0 or 0.0: Less than half the smallest unit shown.
n.a.: Not applicable.

Table 9. Major recipients of bilateral ODA
Net disbursements

Rank	1982/83				1987/88				1992/93			
	Recipient	Current $ million	% of bilateral allocable	Cumulative % of bilateral allocable	Recipient	Current $ million	% of bilateral allocable	Cumulative % of bilateral allocable	Recipient	Current $ million	% of bilateral allocable	Cumulative % of bilateral allocable
1	Tanzania	40.1	20.3	20.3	Tanzania	63.5	15.9	15.9	Tanzania	87.8	17.5	17.5
2	India	33.4	16.9	37.2	India	38.1	9.5	25.4	Uganda	41.2	8.2	25.7
3	Bangladesh	22.6	11.4	48.6	Kenya	31.2	7.8	33.2	Bangladesh	33.0	6.6	32.3
4	Kenya	18.9	9.5	58.1	Bangladesh	30.6	7.7	40.9	Mozambique	29.2	5.8	38.1
5	Sudan	8.5	4.3	62.4	China *	21.3	5.3	46.3	India	29.1	5.8	43.9
6	China	6.8	3.5	65.9	Egypt	20.9	5.2	51.5	Zimbabwe	26.9	5.3	49.2
7	Mozambique	6.7	3.4	69.3	Mozambique	15.4	3.9	55.3	Egypt	24.6	4.9	54.1
8	Zimbabwe	4.9	2.5	71.8	Botswana *	12.8	3.2	58.5	Nicaragua	19.9	4.0	58.1
9	Zambia	4.9	2.5	74.2	Nicaragua	10.9	2.7	61.3	Kenya	18.9	3.8	61.8
10	Lebanon	4.4	2.2	76.5	Yemen *	10.5	2.6	63.9	Zambia	16.6	3.3	65.1
11	Angola	4.1	2.1	78.5	Zimbabwe	10.3	2.6	66.5	Burkina Faso	13.6	2.7	67.8
12	Cameroon	3.6	1.8	80.3	Somalia *	9.1	2.3	68.8	Nepal	12.8	2.5	70.4
13	Thailand	3.6	1.8	82.1	Sudan *	8.6	2.2	70.9	Niger	11.7	2.3	72.7
14	Senegal	3.4	1.7	83.9	Nepal	8.6	2.1	73.1	Ethiopia	11.6	2.3	75.0
15	Egypt	3.4	1.7	85.6	Uganda	8.3	2.1	75.1	Ghana	9.7	1.9	76.9
16	Ethiopia	2.3	1.2	86.7	Malawi *	8.1	2.0	77.2	China *	9.3	1.8	78.8
17	Bolivia	2.1	1.1	87.8	Niger	6.5	1.6	78.8	Bhutan	8.6	1.7	80.5
18	Malawi	2.1	1.1	88.9	Mauritania *	6.4	1.6	80.4	Namibia *	7.8	1.6	82.1
19	Burkina Faso	2.0	1.0	89.9	Sri Lanka *	6.1	1.5	81.9	Thailand *	5.7	1.1	83.2
20	Lesotho	1.9	1.0	90.9	Zambia	5.9	1.5	83.4	Yemen *	5.3	1.1	84.2
	Total bilateral allocable	**197.7**	**100.0**	**100.0**	**Total bilateral allocable**	**399.5**	**100.0**	**100.0**	**Total bilateral allocable**	**502.4**	**100.0**	**100.0**
	Unallocated (additional to total shown)	28.1	14.2		Unallocated (additional to total shown)	68.9	17.2		Unallocated (additional to total shown)	253.3	50.4	
	Memo. item: Total number of recipients:	84			*Memo. item:* Total number of recipients:	75			*Memo. item:* Total number of recipients:	90		

Sign used: * Will be phased out except for mixed credits and NGO activities.

Graph 3. **Distribution by income group of bilateral net disbursements**
1992 constant prices

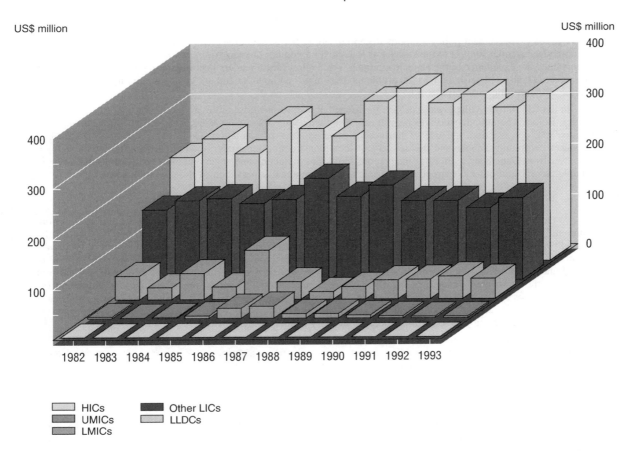

US$ million

US$ million

| 1982 | 1983 | 1984 | 1985 | 1986 | 1987 | 1988 | 1989 | 1990 | 1991 | 1992 | 1993 |

HICs

Other LICs

UMICs

LLDCs

LMICs

Box 3.   **A Danish Country Programme: Uganda**

The following description of projects funded by Denmark is based on a field visit to Kampala in April 1995 by the United States DAC Delegate.

Danish aid emphasizes use of local expertise

A $35 million village project will bring water to four million people. Danish aid provides financial support to pay for the imported construction components and is supporting the construction of pumps, wells, and protected springs in over 7 000 locations. One expatriate engineer supervises Danish input and calls in additional technical expertise as required. The projects are carried out by local communities and local construction firms under the supervision of 300 employees of the Ugandan Government.

In a project to achieve an improved cost-benefit ratio for investments in imported drugs, Danish aid has had to engage more foreign experts, but the tasks of improving training of pharmacists, creating and maintaining drug quality testing services, building new storehouses and manufacturing intravenous solution are much more complex. Furthermore, for the basic purposes of the project, improved drug import policies and distribution systems, substantive expertise is very limited in Uganda. Nevertheless, even in these conditions, emphasis is placed on developing local expertise with a restrained use of foreign experts.

(continued on next page)

(continued)

Danish aid supports decentralisation policy

Ugandan Government policy supports decentralisation, but communities lack resources to respond. DANIDA committed substantial support to the District of Rakai over a number of years to support community priorities. Other donors cited the excellence of the Danish approach which allows local leaders maximum flexibility in realising their aspirations. Danish aid helps address the problems most important to them and has gained credibility as a partner for solving difficult long-term problems.

In the $35 million village water project mentioned above, local communities are taking on significant responsibilities. Before a community receives help in establishing a source for saving water, it must carry out a campaign to promote the construction and use of latrines or other systems of sanitation. Once the community qualifies, it organises community labour and the delivery of local construction materials. In addition, local organisations will take over from Danish aid authorities the responsibility for conducting and supervising the local firms which supply pumps, cement and other construction materials and the technical supervision of the community workers.

Danish aid support training of women in non-traditional skills

A factory for the production of construction materials has brought pride and new motivation to an entire community. At Masese, Uganda, Danish aid is financing an innovative NGO project which has so successfully trained women as carpenters that one of the project's greatest challenges is to replace those lost to private construction firms. The project was originally requested by a community of women who say that they were "prostitutes, drug addicts, and alcoholics who did not even take their children to school." Today, bricks and roof tiles from the construction materials factory have been used to build over two-thirds of the 500 homes in the community. Observers say this was an important factor in overcoming resistance from the males in this traditional community. The factory also produces latrine covers and curved bricks for water cisterns and materials are also sold for use in the construction of Danish-financed elementary schools and elsewhere.

A major constraint in this project, as in other start-ups of small businesses, is cash flow, especially since imported cement is used extensively as the primary input to the manufacturing of the construction materials. Danish authorities have responded pragmatically with contracts to build additional school buildings at nearby localities where they are desperately needed.

Denmark addresses the problem of corruption

In several commodity-import programmes for Uganda, the local authorities have not yet been able to document the delivery of all of the units of drugs or cement financed by Danish aid. The Ugandan authorities stated their respect for Danish tenacity in pursuing this problem. Although many commodities are urgently needed in Uganda, Denmark is now focusing on other forms of assistance for the economy and for local communities, thus minimising exposure to the diversion of goods intended for aid purposes, while providing more effective catalysts for development. Furthermore, Denmark is supporting the Inspector General and the Auditor General of Uganda in their fight against corruption.

Denmark grapples with the issue of salary supplements

Like other donors to Uganda, the Danes supplement the salaries of civil servants who work on programmes supported by development co-operation. Danish aid also co-operates with the overall civil service reform aimed at reducing the phenomenon of "phantom" staff at increasing salaries. These supplements are necessary since Ugandan government wages are still insufficient to keep a family. Donors have agreed on a shadow schedule of compensation, on which to base salary supplement, which works rather imperfectly. A more basic problem, however, is that the dependence of counterpart officials on donor-provided salary supplements is fundamentally unhealthy for the development process and is a serious constraint in Uganda to local "ownership" of development co-operation efforts. Denmark is providing financial support to the major World Bank programme designed to address this issue.

Danish construction firms participate in high-priority infrastructure projects

The selection of infrastructure investments by Denmark is seen by its Ugandan counterparts and other donors as well focused. Danish firms are engaged in a sub-project of the construction of large additional hydroelectric capacity and in upgrading the airport runway and control tower functions at Entebbe airport. Electricity supply is very inadequate and an obvious constraint to development. Upgrading of the airport's performance will open up this landlocked country to more tourism and should offer significant additional opportunity to exports of perishable goods, such as flowers. The Danish contractors were selected on a competitive basis from a short-list of Danish firms. While the economic return on both projects should be excellent, Uganda's overwhelming poverty and debt situation would not permit commercial borrowing for these large projects. Finance was provided on the basis of Danish procurement.

Sectoral distribution

Since the concentration of Danish aid resources is a major issue in the Strategy, bilateral assistance will be concentrated on fewer sectors at the recipient country level. It is stated in the Strategy that all sectors are, *a priori,* eligible for Danish support. The ultimate selection of sectors should be the result of "a qualified dialogue" between donor and recipient. In this context particular emphasis should be placed on sectors where Denmark as a donor country is particularly qualified to provide assistance.

The actual distribution of bilateral ODA commitments by sector is given in Table 10, which also provides a breakdown by region and major recipient countries. For the first time, data which combine the sectoral and geographical distribution of ODA are available for this report. However, as in the case of data on regional distribution of ODA, the validity of these statistics is limited by the large portion – one-third – of unallocated amounts.

Table 10 shows a predominance of Danish bilateral ODA for **public health,** a sector which in 1993 accounted for 34 per cent of allocable commitments. This includes population activities. As indicated in the table, the major recipients of public health support thus defined were in 1993 Bhutan, Egypt, Ghana (where such aid accounted for 79 per cent of total bilateral commitments from Denmark to that country), Mali, and Zambia. In Bhutan and Zambia health support is extended in the form of programme assistance, while in other recipient countries it has been in the form of individual health projects.

Another sector of particular significance in Denmark's bilateral programme is **agriculture.** In Bangladesh, which is a major recipient among Danish programme countries, one-third of bilateral commitments was channelled to that sector in 1993. Activities have been concentrated on integrated rural development – at the initial stage in the areas of agricultural production, fresh water fishing and water resource management. Support has also been extended to road construction and river transport. The substantial amount channelled to the agricultural sector in India forms part of the poverty alleviation aid Denmark extends to that country. In 1993 aid to the agricultural sector accounted for more than half of Danish bilateral ODA to Thailand, mainly in the form of support to dairy production and fishing. In Sub-Saharan Africa more than 80 per cent of bilateral aid to Namibia (which is not a programme country) went to agriculture in the same year; the major share of Danish ODA to that country is channelled through NGOs. Out of the $28.5 million committed to Mozambique in 1993, over 20 per cent went to agriculture, including small-scale fishing.

After public health and agriculture **other social infrastructure,** which in these statistics comprises water supply and sanitation, public administration and development services, is the third sector in importance. Out of bilateral allocable commitments close to 16 per cent were channelled to this sector in 1993. Despite being a programme country, Nepal received a relatively limited bilateral ODA amount, $9 million, of which close to half, 48 per cent, went to other social infrastructure, including support for democratisation, notably an improved system for registration of the electorate, and strengthening of the local administration. In addition to contributions for public health, bilateral ODA extended to Uganda has to a high degree, 31 per cent, been channelled to other social infrastructure, covering support to institutions aimed at strengthening democracy, human rights and women's participation in social and economic life. In particular, aid is financing a reform of the local administration and for the strengthening of the judiciary and the ombudsman system.

C. Terms and conditions of bilateral ODA

Financial terms

Since the adoption of the Plan of Action in 1989, Danish ODA has been provided in grant form. Most of the outstanding debt on earlier aid credits has been forgiven.

Aid financed procurement

With the abolition in 1989 of the administrative distinction between tied and untied assistance a new system of "informal tying" has been introduced. The new system implies that goods and services for ODA-financed development activities can be procured freely in any country provided that at least 50 per cent of total procurement is of Danish origin. This policy is evidently based on the conception that there is a trade-off between the Danish ODA volume and the degree to which Danish resources are employed in the provision of this aid.

Table 10. **Allocable ODA commitments by sectors and main recipients in 1993**

Per cent of total

	Education	Health	Other social infra-structures	Energy	Transport and commu-nications	Agriculture	Industry mining and construc.	Trade, banking, tourism	Import, B.O.P. support	Other and multi-sector	Total bilateral	P.M.: Total $ million
Sub-Saharan Africa	**8.0**	**46.8**	**10.8**	**6.6**	**6.5**	**12.4**	**1.1**	**0.3**	**3.2**	**4.4**	**100.0**	**297.4**
Low-income countries	7.4	51.7	9.9	7.3	7.1	6.7	1.2	0.3	3.5	4.8	100.0	268.9
of which: Burkina Faso	3.2	53.2	9.3	33.2	–	0.2	–	–	–	1.1	100.0	56.0
Ghana	–	79.0	0.5	0.3	16.2	3.1	–	–	–	0.9	100.0	63.7
Guinea	–	61.1	38.9	–	–	–	–	–	–	–	100.0	5.4
Kenya	1.4	28.1	2.8	0.5	34.1	29.0	2.3	–	–	1.8	100.0	21.7
Mali	–	86.0	14.0	–	–	–	–	–	–	–	100.0	24.3
Mozambique	9.1	3.9	2.1	2.1	–	21.8	–	–	32.6	28.4	100.0	28.5
Niger	–	48.1	20.3	–	1.3	16.5	10.1	–	–	3.8	100.0	7.9
Tanzania	28.2	16.2	27.4	0.9	7.7	9.4	–	6.8	–	3.4	100.0	11.7
Uganda	50.0	3.7	30.6	0.0	0.9	–	3.7	–	–	12.0	100.0	10.8
Zambia	1.7	91.0	2.8	0.0	2.2	0.6	0.6	–	–	1.7	100.0	17.8
Lower middle-income countries	13.7	–	19.3	0.0	–	66.7	–	–	–	0.4	100.0	28.5
of which: Namibia	16.9	–	0.9	0.0	–	82.3	–	–	–	0.4	100.0	23.1
North-Africa and Middle East	**2.4**	**56.3**	**18.0**	**1.2**	**–**	**–**	**18.4**	**–**	**–**	**3.7**	**100.0**	**24.5**
Low-income countries	2.5	56.1	18.0	1.2	–	–	18.4	–	–	3.3	100.0	24.4
of which: Egypt	3.0	49.2	19.3	1.5	–	–	22.8	–	–	4.1	100.0	19.7
Asia	**13.2**	**17.5**	**20.9**	**1.4**	**14.3**	**27.4**	**3.5**	**0.1**	**0.5**	**1.2**	**100.0**	**164.5**
Low-income countries	12.3	17.3	23.2	0.3	14.8	26.9	3.5	0.1	0.6	1.2	100.0	142.5
of which: Bangladesh	0.5	11.8	21.9	0.5	33.2	31.5	–	–	–	0.6	100.0	62.6
Bhutan	–	68.8	17.3	–	1.5	6.4	4.0	–	–	2.5	100.0	20.2
India	22.3	4.0	26.2	–	–	42.1	4.9	0.3	–	0.3	100.0	32.8
Indonesia	75.9	–	0.9	–	–	3.4	19.8	–	–	–	100.0	11.6
Nepal	8.5	3.2	47.9	1.1	–	33.0	–	–	–	6.4	100.0	9.4
Lower middle-income countries	19.1	18.6	6.4	8.6	11.4	30.9	3.6	0.5	–	0.9	100.0	22.0
of which: Mongolia	–	–	–	31.4	47.1	3.9	15.7	–	–	2.0	100.0	5.1
Thailand	33.1	14.2	–	–	–	51.2	–	–	–	0.8	100.0	12.7
America	**3.1**	**2.2**	**30.0**	**4.2**	**33.3**	**10.7**	**–**	**0.2**	**0.4**	**15.4**	**100.0**	**45.6**
Low-income countries	0.8	–	28.9	5.2	41.1	6.0	–	0.3	0.5	16.9	100.0	36.7
of which: Nicaragua	0.8	–	29.0	5.2	41.4	6.0	–	0.3	–	17.0	100.0	36.5
Lower middle-income countries	12.4	11.2	34.8	–	1.1	30.3	–	–	–	9.0	100.0	8.9
Total bilateral allocable	**8.9**	**34.3**	**15.9**	**4.5**	**10.9**	**16.3**	**2.5**	**0.2**	**2.0**	**4.3**	**100.0**	**532.0**
Memo items:												
Least developed countries	6.0	39.7	17.4	7.2	8.2	12.2	0.8	0.3	3.7	4.6	100.0	275.2
Other low-income countries	11.1	34.6	13.6	1.3	16.7	12.6	5.3	0.1	0.1	4.5	100.0	197.3
Lower middle-income countries	15.5	8.7	17.0	3.2	4.4	47.9	1.3	0.2	–	2.0	100.0	59.5
Upper middle-income countries	–	–	–	–	–	–	–	–	–	–	–	–
High-income countries	–	–	–	–	–	–	–	–	–	–	–	–
Unallocated (additional to total shown)	3.2	3.8	5.7	0.6	2.0	10.4	1.1	–	–	73.2	100.0	311.0

Sign used: – Nil.
Sources: Creditor Reporting System and DAC Statistics Table 5 A.

While the policy takes into account the interests of the Danish private sector, the principle has been established that products and services purchased in Denmark should only be taken into consideration to the extent that they are competitive with regard to technology, price and quality. Where Danish goods and services are not considered to be competitive, offers/tenders should be invited from other countries. It may be useful to recall in this context the definition of untied ODA, as agreed among DAC countries. According to *"DAC Principles for Effective Aid"*, OECD, Paris, 1992, *New Measures in the Field of Tied Aid,* p. 125, "... Untied ODA is defined as loans and grants which are freely and fully available to finance procurement from substantially all developing countries and from OECD countries. For transactions to qualify as untied..., the donor has to inform the recipient at the time of the aid offer, clearly and explicitly, of the countries which are eligible for procurement."

The "50 per cent return" to Denmark from bilateral aid expenditure is a political target set by Parliament. It is measured *ex post* on the overall outcome of aid disbursements and is therefore only indirectly related to the tying status (in DAC terminology) of Danish aid. Untied ODA as defined by the DAC can also contribute to the attainment of the 50 per cent target, if internationally competitive Danish suppliers are awarded aid-financed contracts. Questions to be discussed in the course of current DAC-work on these issues are how to achieve transparency, how to clarify policy and practice, and in particular how to ensure the effective untying of aid in the context of DAC rules and disciplines.

According to the 1993 figures, there is a wide discrepancy between the objective of 50 per cent of bilateral ODA projects and programmes to be procured in Denmark and the actual procurement ratio, which in that year accounted for only 27 per cent. If the entire bilateral ODA programme is taken into consideration, *i.e.* including technical co-operation, the reception of refugees, etc., goods and services of Danish origin account for a much higher ratio, some 55 per cent in 1992, 52 per cent in 1993 and 50 per cent in 1994.

The Danish authorities consider that actual procurement in Denmark has been rather limited because of the prominent position given to poverty alleviation in the ODA programme. In previous years Denmark to a considerable extent had recourse to import support in its ODA programme to ensure a sufficient portion of procurement in Denmark. With the growing importance of structural adjustment arrangements, import support has gradually been replaced with untied balance-of-payments support.

Chapter IV

Denmark's Co-operation with India

In January 1995, at Denmark's invitation, an OECD Secretariat team visited selected Indian development programmes supported by Danish aid. The visit covered projects in the State of Tamil Nadu and in Delhi and included discussions with the Royal Danish Embassy. In addition, the mission team met representatives of the European Commission, World Bank, UNDP and several UN agencies at their field offices and paid visits to several departments of the Government of India (GOI).

A. India's present situation

India is in the middle of far reaching reforms, which began in late 1991. A programme of stabilization and economic reform measures have already brought about considerable growth of trade, foreign investment and foreign exchange reserves. Economic growth has been restored to around 4 per cent in real terms, and real GNP/capita growth has been 3 per cent between 1985 and 1993. However, major unfinished business remains on the reform agenda. The rationalisation of the public sector, concerning both state-owned enterprises and public administration at Union and State level, is one area of concern, although a politically sensitive one. Other areas in need of improvement are: capacity of middle-level administrations in the Union States for the provision of basic social services in rural areas; physical infrastructure (transport, telecommunication, and power generation/distribution). Moreover, poverty is pervasive in India: about 70 per cent of Indians live in rural areas, a great number of whom below the official (Indian) poverty line. Rural poverty, in turn, is the consequence of low productivity of the rural labour force.

India has been receiving substantial amounts of foreign assistance during the last decade. The provision of quick disbursing funds for import support in 1991 and 1992 – the donors' contribution to the stabilization programme – resulted in receipts of around \$2 billion annually for each of those two years. Disbursements in 1993 of \$1.5 billion corresponded to the longer-term average. While this aid volume is relatively small compared to the size of the Indian economy (less than 1 per cent of GNP), the Indian authorities have often had difficulty in absorbing all of it.

In the view of the Indian Government fast disbursing aid is presently not required because of substantial improvements of the external account but foreign assistance remains critical for infrastructure and social sectors. Indian officials have expressed the expectation that such support, particularly for health services and environmental protection which India had somewhat neglected in the past, will be required for a transition period of five to ten years.

B. Danish assistance to India

The Danish programme seems to respond well to Indian needs as perceived jointly by Denmark and the Indian authorities. As indicated in Denmark's 1994 ''Country Strategy for India'', the overall objective of Danish assistance for India is poverty alleviation, covering projects in agriculture, health, and water and sanitation. In general, Danish assistance is purpose-oriented and helps to fill gaps in India's system of social service delivery. The way in which the programme is managed also shows evidence of mutually satisfactory co-operation. In an approach combining co-operation with the authorities, in particular at state and district level, and with grassroot target groups, Danish experts and other locally engaged and expatriate personnel of the Danish programme tend to play an effective, if discreet, role as counsellors, rather than project managers. Active participation of official institutions and target groups is contributing to the sustainability of the programmes supported.

While ODA from DAC countries for India increased from $0.6 billion on average in 1982-85 to $1.1 billion in 1990-93, the Danish share in the total volume declined from 5 to 3 per cent (see table below "DAC countries' ODA to India"). As spelled out in the 1994 Strategy for Danish Assistance for India, Denmark has reduced its assistance also in absolute terms from $62 million in 1992 to $35 million in 1993, and a further reduction of 25 per cent by 1998 is planned. The reasons for this include the growth of the Indian economy in recent years, but India will nevertheless remain on the list of 20 Danish programme countries.

DAC countries' ODA to India

In per cent of total bilateral[1]

1982-85		1990-93	
Germany	18	Japan	37
United Kingdom	18	Germany	19
Netherlands	11	United Kingdom	11
Japan	9	Netherlands	9
Sweden	8	Sweden	8
United States	8	France	5
Canada	8	Denmark	3
France	7	Switzerland	3
Denmark	5	Canada	2
Norway	4	Norway	2
Total DAC	100	Total DAC	100
	($593 million)		($1 136 million)

1. Four-year averages.

At field level, Danish assistance is managed by several officials and local experts at the Embassy in New Delhi, including active participation by the Ambassador. In addition, each of the pilot programmes is being supported by a local DANIDA team of experts. These teams provide professional advice and liaise between target groups and Indian authorities as well as between the programmes and the Embassy and/or DANIDA headquarters in Copenhagen. Many of the members of these support teams are Indian nationals, and some are expatriates from Denmark or from other countries such as the Netherlands. The personnel input in Danish aid management may appear relatively costly, but it seems to be justified by the quality and effectiveness of the programmes.

Box 4. **Tamil Nadu Women in Agriculture (TANWA)**

After a first phase (1986-93), covering only six out of 23 Districts, TANWA is now extended into the entire State and will have provided training, by the year 2001, to about 75 000 women from small and marginal farms. By encouraging these women to share their new skills in agricultural technology with other women of the neighbourhood, it is hoped that eventually the number of trained farm women will reach 750 000 in Tamil Nadu.

The extension of the programme into its second phase (TANWA-II) has been decided by the State authorities, the GOI and the Danish authorities on the basis of an evaluation of the results of TANWA-I. One of the positive results of this earlier phase was the creation of a pool of 30 qualified women agricultural officers capable of teaching these skills to women with low literacy attainment.

Denmark is contributing about $10 million as grants to TANWA-II, covering the cost of the office of a DANIDA advisor in Madras and the salaries and other costs for project staff (10 at state level, about 300 at district level). The Government of Tamil Nadu, through its Department of Agriculture, will take over the cost of project staff from the fifth year of TANWA-II. With similar farm-training projects supported by Denmark in three other Union States, a main issue in the Indo-Danish dialogue is how to take account of the needs of women farmers in India's agricultural policy. To ensure sustainability of the results achieved by the four Danish pilot projects, and to expand them into other Union States, this dialogue presently involves the GOI and respective State Governments. The recent Indian initiative to start similar projects in nine other States following the concept of DANIDA's projects would indicate that the GOI's policy with regard to farm women has been significantly influenced by the DANIDA projects.

The characteristics of Danish aid to India are well illustrated by a programme concerning the training of women in agricultural activities (see Box 4). With a grassroots, participatory approach, long-term commitment, and shared donor-recipient responsibility for input and management, the project aims at improving the knowledge and skills of women who are small-scale farmers, thereby improving crop yield, and providing additional income and higher social standing for these women and their families. The programme and the resulting enhanced independence of women farmers has hitherto been well received by the local community, including the male population. It is being replicated in other Indian States. In the sector of environmental protection, Denmark is providing substantial support for the establishment of an Environment Action Plan in the Union State of Karnataka (see Box 5).

Box 5.   **Environment Action Plan in the State of Karnataka, India**

The expected increase in economic activities, combined with considerable population growth in the Dakshina Kannada district, affects natural resources and the ecological balance in the State to an unprecedented extent. Denmark has therefore agreed to allocate $4.3 million for the elaboration of an environment action plan.

Given that environmental degradation is the result of complex processes, the action plan will cover a wide range of actions, all contributing towards sustainable development. The plan will help, in particular, to strengthen the authorities' capacity to collect data and assess the environmental situation generally, map out the use of cultivated land, mobilise popular participation in solving environmental problems, and manage the rehabilitation of particularly polluted areas.

Among the activities planned are training of personnel, the introduction and use of economic parameters, information campaigns, renovation of existing facilities, development and use of improved technologies and waste recycling.

In the area of health care, Denmark is supporting a programme aimed at creating health centres at village level in which the local population is involved through donations of land, money and voluntary labour. The programme, which is integrated into the public health administration, fills a gap in the provision of services for the rural population and is therefore readily accepted both by the target groups and the administration. It is to be hoped that the lessons from this pilot project can be applied to rural areas in other parts of India.

C.   Critical issues

Denmark encounters difficulties in terminating some of its programmes in India. These are often extended through several phases with additional funds being provided each time, not always backed up by a thorough assessment of results. While fully appreciating the difficulties for a relatively small donor to manage aid programmes in a country like India with its long-standing bureaucratic traditions, Denmark does not always seem to be able to create the conditions for self-supporting development. Reasons for this may be found in programme preparation, in particular sometimes over-optimistic appraisal of the time required to reach sustainability. An in-depth evaluation of the effects of these programmes or the sectors concerned, at district or state level, would be required to shed light on this situation. However, as a positive aspect of such prolongation of aid programmes, the learning effect for donor and recipient can be mentioned. DANIDA and its Indian counterparts are thus able to draw lessons from good or bad experiences.

Although the development of an Indian private sector is part of DANIDA's aid objectives, no clear vision of how to reach it seems yet to exist. Denmark intends to develop a strategy for private sector development in India which is supposed to take effect from 1997, in parallel with the planned reduction of the bilateral ODA volume. While mixed credits are expected to be used in this context, it is understood that assistance for social sectors needs to be maintained, given the fact that a large number of Indian poor are still profiting very little, if at all, from the ongoing economic reforms. The objectives of the country strategy, including the forms of aid, may need further elaboration and clarification to assure an even better impact of Danish assistance on India's development. In the event, it will be essential for Danish aid to maintain its focus on poverty alleviation if India should remain one of the Danish programme countries, given the relatively small amounts of ODA available for the country.

Press Release of the DAC Aid Review of Denmark

The Development Assistance Committee (DAC) of the OECD reviewed Denmark's development co-operation programme and policies on 31st May 1995. The Danish Delegation was headed by Mr. Ole Lønsmann Poulsen, State Secretary, Ministry of Foreign Affairs. The examining Member countries were the Netherlands and the United States.

The Chair of the DAC, Mr. James H. Michel, summarised the main points discussed in the review:

a) Denmark's development co-operation programme inspires confidence and optimism. The way in which the programme is conducted and the results it is achieving can help to dispel doubts about the role of aid and its effectiveness. Denmark has made impressive policy decisions in response to a changing global situation, including timely efforts to improve the coherence of Danish policies toward developing countries. It is making excellent progress in the implementation of strategies to carry out those policy decisions.

b) The DAC analysed the Danish development Strategy "A Developing World", which was adopted by the Government and endorsed by Parliament in 1994. The Committee found that the Strategy, while adjusting Danish policies to the new global context and further improving coherence among these policies, introduces several noteworthy innovations in both bilateral and multilateral co-operation.

c) It is envisaged to further concentrate bilateral official development assistance (ODA) on a limited number of poor recipient countries and on a few sectors most relevant for recipient country needs and Danish capabilities. Aid statistics show that Danish bilateral assistance is already almost entirely – over 90 per cent – reserved for least developed and other low-income countries, mainly in Sub-Saharan Africa. The Committee noted with particular interest that the new Strategy contemplates the formulation of a country programme for each primary recipient, with a strong element of participation by partners in recipient country administrations and civil society in the design and implementation of those country programmes.

d) Denmark will in future strengthen its selective approach to multilateral co-operation. This approach, termed "active multilateralism", will be based on Danish efforts to assess, and improve, efficiency and effectiveness of international aid institutions. The Committee noted with appreciation that Denmark is among the few DAC Members who have started to monitor and evaluate the effectiveness of multilateral aid activities.

e) The DAC was impressed by the persistent high level of Danish ODA in recent years, with a ODA/GNP ratios of 1.03 per cent in both 1993 and 1994 (amounting to $1.45 billion in this latter year). This remarkable performance is strongly supported by Danish public opinion and political circles. A relatively high share – around 45 per cent – of this aid volume is channelled into multilateral activities.

f) The Committee took note of Denmark's intention to strengthen its assistance for activities in the area of population policy in the context of comprehensive health sector support programmes that integrate mother and child health care and family planning with a focus on helping partner countries to increase the institutional and operational capacity of their health systems.

g) The Delegation informed the DAC about experience with the reorganised structure of the aid administration. The merger of DANIDA, the former aid agency, with the Ministry of Foreign Affairs in 1991 and the decentralisation of aid management responsibilities to Danish embassies, has underlined the importance of professional development knowledge and institutional memory. In this context, the Committee acknowledged particularly Danish efforts to strengthen the management capacity of recipient administrations.

h) The Committee discussed the impact of the present Danish regime of ODA financed procurement on the effectiveness of Danish aid. This discussion also covered the attempt of the aid authorities to promote and encourage private sector linkages between Denmark and recipient countries.

Denmark: Comparative aid performance

	ODA net disbursements 1993 — $ million	ODA net disbursements 1993 — % of GNP	Average annual growth in real terms 1987/88-1992/93 a	Grant element of ODA commitments 1993 b (%)	ODA appropriation as share of central government budget (%) 1991	Share of multilateral aid 1992/93 c — % of ODA	Share of multilateral aid 1992/93 c — % of GNP	ODA to LLDCs Bilateral and imputed multilateral 1993 — % of ODA	ODA to LLDCs Bilateral and imputed multilateral 1993 — % of GNP
Australia	954	0.35	0.8	100.0	1.3	26.1	0.09	19.9	0.07
Austria	544	0.30	11.0	88.2	0.6	24.5	0.07	20.3	0.06
Belgium	808	0.39	-0.0	(99.4)	0.9	19.9 (38.8)	0.08 (0.15)	22.7	0.09
Canada	2 373	0.45	-0.3	99.5	1.9	32.4	0.15	23.7	0.11
Denmark	**1 340**	**1.03**	**4.3**	**100.0**	**3.2**	**38.3 (44.7)**	**0.39 (0.46)**	**35.4**	**0.37**
Finland	355	0.45	-1.7	98.5	2.0	33.6	0.19	26.4	0.12
France	7 915	0.63	3.7	(89.8)	3.2	12.3 (23.0)	0.08 (0.15)	23.6	0.15
Germany	6 954	0.36	4.1	93.1	2.1	16.9 (32.9)	0.06 (0.12)	27.1	0.10
Ireland	81	0.20	4.5	100.0	0.6	18.5 (55.4)	0.03 (0.10)	42.1	0.08
Italy	3 043	0.31	-0.6	97.7	0.6	23.0 (39.1)	0.08 (0.13)	26.5	0.08
Japan	11 259	0.27	1.9	79.0	1.3	26.7	0.08	17.4	0.05
Luxembourg	50	0.35	16.6	..	1.2	16.1 (39.0)	0.05 (0.12)	33.2	0.12
Netherlands	2 525	0.82	-0.1	100.0	(2.7)	21.3 (30.7)	0.18 (0.26)	26.9	0.22
New Zealand	98	0.25	0.0	100.0	0.5	24.6	0.06	19.6	0.05
Norway	1 014	1.01	1.0	99.6	2.0	35.8	0.39	43.8	0.44
Portugal	248	0.29	20.5	100.0	0.3	4.4 (21.1)	0.01 (0.07)	76.4	0.22
Spain	1 213	0.25	31.4	(84.8)	0.6	5.9 (28.8)	0.02 (0.08)	12.0	0.03
Sweden	1 769	0.99	3.0	100.0	2.7	26.5	0.27	33.8	0.33
Switzerland	793	0.33	5.8	100.0	3.1	32.1	0.27	32.9	0.11
United Kingdom	2 920	0.31	1.8	(100.0)	1.2	24.7 (47.7)	0.08 (0.15)	26.7	0.08
United States	10 149	0.16	-1.0	99.2	(0.8)	30.5	0.05	22.2	0.04
Total DAC	56 405	0.31	1.6	91.8	(1.2)	24.1 (31.3)	0.08 (0.10)	24.0	0.07
Memo.: Unweighted average		0.45	(1.6)						

..: Indicates that data are not available.

a) For 1992 the total excludes forgiveness of non-ODA debt which is however included in individual donor disbursements as follows:
   i) Export credits: Australia $4 million, Austria $25 million, Belgium $30 million, France $109 million, Germany $620 million, Japan $32 million, the Netherlands $11 million, Norway $47 million, Sweden $7 million and the United Kingdom $90 million.
   ii) Military debt: United States $894 million.

b) Excluding debt reorganisation.

c) Excluding contributions to the EC; in brackets including contributions to the EC.

Net ODA from DAC countries in 1993

As % of GNP

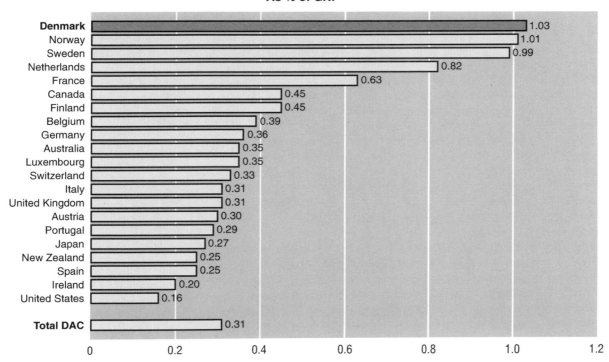

Denmark	1.03
Norway	1.01
Sweden	0.99
Netherlands	0.82
France	0.63
Canada	0.45
Finland	0.45
Belgium	0.39
Germany	0.36
Australia	0.35
Luxembourg	0.35
Switzerland	0.33
Italy	0.31
United Kingdom	0.31
Austria	0.30
Portugal	0.29
Japan	0.27
New Zealand	0.25
Spain	0.25
Ireland	0.20
United States	0.16
Total DAC	0.31

$ billion

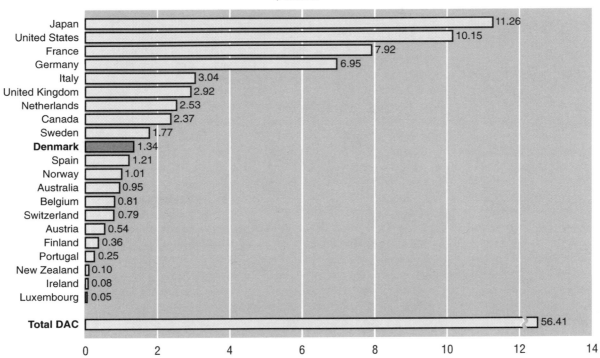

Japan	11.26
United States	10.15
France	7.92
Germany	6.95
Italy	3.04
United Kingdom	2.92
Netherlands	2.53
Canada	2.37
Sweden	1.77
Denmark	1.34
Spain	1.21
Norway	1.01
Australia	0.95
Belgium	0.81
Switzerland	0.79
Austria	0.54
Finland	0.36
Portugal	0.25
New Zealand	0.10
Ireland	0.08
Luxembourg	0.05
Total DAC	56.41

MAIN SALES OUTLETS OF OECD PUBLICATIONS
PRINCIPAUX POINTS DE VENTE DES PUBLICATIONS DE L'OCDE

ARGENTINA – ARGENTINE
Carlos Hirsch S.R.L.
Galería Güemes, Florida 165, 4° Piso
1333 Buenos Aires   Tel. (1) 331.1787 y 331.2391
                     Telefax: (1) 331.1787

AUSTRALIA – AUSTRALIE
D.A. Information Services
648 Whitehorse Road, P.O.B 163
Mitcham, Victoria 3132   Tel. (03) 873.4411
                              Telefax: (03) 873.5679

AUSTRIA – AUTRICHE
Gerold & Co.
Graben 31
Wien I   Tel. (0222) 533.50.14
                  Telefax: (0222) 512.47.31.29

BELGIUM – BELGIQUE
Jean De Lannoy
Avenue du Roi 202 Koningslaan
B-1060 Bruxelles   Tel. (02) 538.51.69/538.08.41
                         Telefax: (02) 538.08.41

CANADA
Renouf Publishing Company Ltd.
1294 Algoma Road
Ottawa, ON K1B 3W8   Tel. (613) 741.4333
                             Telefax: (613) 741.5439
Stores:
61 Sparks Street
Ottawa, ON K1P 5R1   Tel. (613) 238.8985
211 Yonge Street
Toronto, ON M5B 1M4   Tel. (416) 363.3171
                             Telefax: (416)363.59.63

Les Éditions La Liberté Inc.
3020 Chemin Sainte-Foy
Sainte-Foy, PQ G1X 3V6   Tel. (418) 658.3763
                             Telefax: (418) 658.3763

Federal Publications Inc.
165 University Avenue, Suite 701
Toronto, ON M5H 3B8   Tel. (416) 860.1611
                             Telefax: (416) 860.1608

Les Publications Fédérales
1185 Université
Montréal, QC H3B 3A7   Tel. (514) 954.1633
                             Telefax: (514) 954.1635

CHINA – CHINE
China National Publications Import
Export Corporation (CNPIEC)
16 Gongti E. Road, Chaoyang District
P.O. Box 88 or 50
Beijing 100704 PR   Tel. (01) 506.6688
                             Telefax: (01) 506.3101

CHINESE TAIPEI – TAIPEI CHINOIS
Good Faith Worldwide Int'l. Co. Ltd.
9th Floor, No. 118, Sec. 2
Chung Hsiao E. Road
Taipei   Tel. (02) 391.7396/391.7397
                         Telefax: (02) 394.9176

CZECH REPUBLIC – RÉPUBLIQUE TCHÈQUE
Artia Pegas Press Ltd.
Narodni Trida 25
POB 825
111 21 Praha 1   Tel. 26.65.68
                             Telefax: 26.20.81

DENMARK – DANEMARK
Munksgaard Book and Subscription Service
35, Nørre Søgade, P.O. Box 2148
DK-1016 København K   Tel. (33) 12.85.70
                         Telefax: (33) 12.93.87

EGYPT – ÉGYPTE
Middle East Observer
41 Sherif Street
Cairo   Tel. 392.6919
                             Telefax: 360-6804

FINLAND – FINLANDE
Akateeminen Kirjakauppa
Keskuskatu 1, P.O. Box 128
00100 Helsinki
Subscription Services/Agence d'abonnements :
P.O. Box 23
00371 Helsinki   Tel. (358 0) 121 4416
                             Telefax: (358 0) 121.4450

FRANCE
OECD/OCDE
Mail Orders/Commandes par correspondance:
2, rue André-Pascal
75775 Paris Cedex 16   Tel. (33-1) 45.24.82.00
                             Telefax: (33-1) 49.10.42.76
                             Telex: 640048 OCDE
Internet: Compte.PUBSINQ @ oecd.org
Orders via Minitel, France only/
Commandes par Minitel, France exclusivement :
36 15 OCDE
OECD Bookshop/Librairie de l'OCDE :
33, rue Octave-Feuillet
75016 Paris   Tel. (33-1) 45.24.81.81
                                  (33-1) 45.24.81.67
Documentation Française
29, quai Voltaire
75007 Paris   Tel. 40.15.70.00
Gibert Jeune (Droit-Économie)
6, place Saint-Michel
75006 Paris   Tel. 43.25.91.19
Librairie du Commerce International
10, avenue d'Iéna
75016 Paris   Tel. 40.73.34.60
Librairie Dunod
Université Paris-Dauphine
Place du Maréchal de Lattre de Tassigny
75016 Paris   Tel. (1) 44.05.40.13
Librairie Lavoisier
11, rue Lavoisier
75008 Paris   Tel. 42.65.39.95
Librairie L.G.D.J. - Montchrestien
20, rue Soufflot
75005 Paris   Tel. 46.33.89.85
Librairie des Sciences Politiques
30, rue Saint-Guillaume
75007 Paris   Tel. 45.48.36.02
P.U.F.
49, boulevard Saint-Michel
75005 Paris   Tel. 43.25.83.40
Librairie de l'Université
12a, rue Nazareth
13100 Aix-en-Provence   Tel. (16) 42.26.18.08
Documentation Française
165, rue Garibaldi
69003 Lyon   Tel. (16) 78.63.32.23
Librairie Decitre
29, place Bellecour
69002 Lyon   Tel. (16) 72.40.54.54
Librairie Sauramps
Le Triangle
34967 Montpellier Cedex 2 Tel. (16) 67.58.85.15
                           Tekefax: (16) 67.58.27.36

GERMANY – ALLEMAGNE
OECD Publications and Information Centre
August-Bebel-Allee 6
D-53175 Bonn   Tel. (0228) 959.120
                             Telefax: (0228) 959.12.17

GREECE – GRÈCE
Librairie Kauffmann
Mavrokordatou 9
106 78 Athens   Tel. (01) 32.55.321
                             Telefax: (01) 32.30.320

HONG-KONG
Swindon Book Co. Ltd.
Astoria Bldg. 3F
34 Ashley Road, Tsimshatsui
Kowloon, Hong Kong   Tel. 2376.2062
                             Telefax: 2376.0685

HUNGARY – HONGRIE
Euro Info Service
Margitsziget, Európa Ház
1138 Budapest   Tel. (1) 111.62.16
                             Telefax: (1) 111.60.61

ICELAND – ISLANDE
Mál Mog Menning
Laugavegi 18, Pósthólf 392
121 Reykjavik   Tel. (1) 552.4240
                             Telefax: (1) 562.3523

INDIA – INDE
Oxford Book and Stationery Co.
Scindia House
New Delhi 110001   Tel. (11) 331.5896/5308
                             Telefax: (11) 332.5993
17 Park Street
Calcutta 700016   Tel. 240832

INDONESIA – INDONÉSIE
Pdii-Lipi
P.O. Box 4298
Jakarta 12042   Tel. (21) 573.34.67
                             Telefax: (21) 573.34.67

IRELAND – IRLANDE
Government Supplies Agency
Publications Section
4/5 Harcourt Road
Dublin 2   Tel. 661.31.11
                             Telefax: 475.27.60

ISRAEL
Praedicta
5 Shatner Street
P.O. Box 34030
Jerusalem 91430   Tel. (2) 52.84.90/1/2
                             Telefax: (2) 52.84.93
R.O.Y. International
P.O. Box 13056
Tel Aviv 61130   Tel. (3) 546 1423
                             Telefax: (3) 546 1442
Palestinian Authority/Middle East:
INDEX Information Services
P.O.B. 19502
Jerusalem   Tel. (2) 27.12.19
                             Telefax: (2) 27.16.34

ITALY – ITALIE
Libreria Commissionaria Sansoni
Via Duca di Calabria 1/1
50125 Firenze   Tel. (055) 64.54.15
                             Telefax: (055) 64.12.57
Via Bartolini 29
20155 Milano   Tel. (02) 36.50.83
Editrice e Libreria Herder
Piazza Montecitorio 120
00186 Roma   Tel. 679.46.28
                             Telefax: 678.47.51
Libreria Hoepli
Via Hoepli 5
20121 Milano   Tel. (02) 86.54.46
                             Telefax: (02) 805.28.86
Libreria Scientifica
Dott. Lucio de Biasio 'Aeiou'
Via Coronelli, 6
20146 Milano   Tel. (02) 48.95.45.52
                             Telefax: (02) 48.95.45.48

JAPAN – JAPON
OECD Publications and Information Centre
Landic Akasaka Building
2-3-4 Akasaka, Minato-ku
Tokyo 107   Tel. (81.3) 3586.2016
                             Telefax: (81.3) 3584.7929

KOREA – CORÉE
Kyobo Book Centre Co. Ltd.
P.O. Box 1658, Kwang Hwa Moon
Seoul   Tel. 730.78.91
                             Telefax: 735.00.30

MALAYSIA – MALAISIE
University of Malaya Bookshop
University of Malaya
P.O. Box 1127, Jalan Pantai Baru
59700 Kuala Lumpur
Malaysia   Tel. 756.5000/756.5425
                            Telefax: 756.3246

MEXICO – MEXIQUE
Revistas y Periodicos Internacionales S.A. de C.V.
Florencia 57 - 1004
Mexico, D.F. 06600   Tel. 207.81.00
                           Telefax: 208.39.79

NETHERLANDS – PAYS-BAS
SDU Uitgeverij Plantijnstraat
Externe Fondsen
Postbus 20014
2500 EA's-Gravenhage   Tel. (070) 37.89.880
Voor bestellingen: Telefax: (070) 34.75.778

NEW ZEALAND
NOUVELLE-ZÉLANDE
GPLegislation Services
P.O. Box 12418
Thorndon, Wellington   Tel. (04) 496.5655
                           Telefax: (04) 496.5698

NORWAY – NORVÈGE
Narvesen Info Center – NIC
Bertrand Narvesens vei 2
P.O. Box 6125 Etterstad
0602 Oslo 6   Tel. (022) 57.33.00
                           Telefax: (022) 68.19.01

PAKISTAN
Mirza Book Agency
65 Shahrah Quaid-E-Azam
Lahore 54000   Tel. (42) 353.601
                           Telefax: (42) 231.730

PHILIPPINE – PHILIPPINES
International Book Center
5th Floor, Filipinas Life Bldg.
Ayala Avenue
Metro Manila   Tel. 81.96.76
                           Telex 23312 RHP PH

PORTUGAL
Livraria Portugal
Rua do Carmo 70-74
Apart. 2681
1200 Lisboa   Tel. (01) 347.49.82/5
                           Telefax: (01) 347.02.64

SINGAPORE – SINGAPOUR
Gower Asia Pacific Pte Ltd.
Golden Wheel Building
41, Kallang Pudding Road, No. 04-03
Singapore 1334   Tel. 741.5166
                           Telefax: 742.9356

SPAIN – ESPAGNE
Mundi-Prensa Libros S.A.
Castelló 37, Apartado 1223
Madrid 28001   Tel. (91) 431.33.99
                           Telefax: (91) 575.39.98

Libreria Internacional AEDOS
Consejo de Ciento 391
08009 – Barcelona   Tel. (93) 488.30.09
                           Telefax: (93) 487.76.59

Llibreria de la Generalitat
Palau Moja
Rambla dels Estudis, 118
08002 – Barcelona
                  (Subscripcions) Tel. (93) 318.80.12
                  (Publicacions) Tel. (93) 302.67.23
                           Telefax: (93) 412.18.54

SRI LANKA
Centre for Policy Research
c/o Colombo Agencies Ltd.
No. 300-304, Galle Road
Colombo 3   Tel. (1) 574240, 573551-2
                           Telefax: (1) 575394, 510711

SWEDEN – SUÈDE
Fritzes Customer Service
S–106 47 Stockholm   Tel. (08) 690.90.90
                           Telefax: (08) 20.50.21

Subscription Agency/Agence d'abonnements :
Wennergren-Williams Info AB
P.O. Box 1305
171 25 Solna   Tel. (08) 705.97.50
                           Telefax: (08) 27.00.71

SWITZERLAND – SUISSE
Maditec S.A. (Books and Periodicals - Livres
et périodiques)
Chemin des Palettes 4
Case postale 266
1020 Renens VD 1   Tel. (021) 635.08.65
                           Telefax: (021) 635.07.80

Librairie Payot S.A.
4, place Pépinet
CP 3212
1002 Lausanne   Tel. (021) 341.33.47
                           Telefax: (021) 341.33.45

Librairie Unilivres
6, rue de Candolle
1205 Genève   Tel. (022) 320.26.23
                           Telefax: (022) 329.73.18

Subscription Agency/Agence d'abonnements :
Dynapresse Marketing S.A.
38 avenue Vibert
1227 Carouge   Tel. (022) 308.07.89
                           Telefax: (022) 308.07.99

See also – Voir aussi :
OECD Publications and Information Centre
August-Bebel-Allee 6
D-53175 Bonn (Germany)   Tel. (0228) 959.120
                           Telefax: (0228) 959.12.17

THAILAND – THAÏLANDE
Suksit Siam Co. Ltd.
113, 115 Fuang Nakhon Rd.
Opp. Wat Rajbopith
Bangkok 10200   Tel. (662) 225.9531/2
                           Telefax: (662) 222.5188

TURKEY – TURQUIE
Kültür Yayinlari Is-Türk Ltd. Sti.
Atatürk Bulvari No. 191/Kat 13
Kavaklidere/Ankara   Tel. 428.11.40 Ext. 2458
Dolmabahce Cad. No. 29
Besiktas/Istanbul   Tel. (312) 260 7188
                           Telex: (312) 418 29 46

UNITED KINGDOM – ROYAUME-UNI
HMSO
Gen. enquiries   Tel. (171) 873 8496
Postal orders only:
P.O. Box 276, London SW8 5DT
Personal Callers HMSO Bookshop
49 High Holborn, London WC1V 6HB
                           Telefax: (171) 873 8416
Branches at: Belfast, Birmingham, Bristol,
Edinburgh, Manchester

UNITED STATES – ÉTATS-UNIS
OECD Publications and Information Center
2001 L Street N.W., Suite 650
Washington, D.C. 20036-4910 Tel. (202) 785.6323
                           Telefax: (202) 785.0350

VENEZUELA
Libreria del Este
Avda F. Miranda 52, Aptdo. 60337
Edificio Galipán
Caracas 106   Tel. 951.1705/951.2307/951.1297
                           Telegram: Libreste Caracas

Subscription to OECD periodicals may also be
placed through main subscription agencies.

Les abonnements aux publications périodiques de
l'OCDE peuvent être souscrits auprès des
principales agences d'abonnement.

Orders and inquiries from countries where Distribu-
tors have not yet been appointed should be sent to:
OECD Publications Service, 2 rue André-Pascal,
75775 Paris Cedex 16, France.

Les commandes provenant de pays où l'OCDE n'a
pas encore désigné de distributeur peuvent être
adressées à : OCDE, Service des Publications,
2, rue André-Pascal, 75775 Paris Cedex 16, France.

7-1995

OECD PUBLICATIONS, 2 rue André-Pascal, 75775 PARIS CEDEX 16
PRINTED IN FRANCE
(43 95 10 1) ISBN 92-64-14581-8 – No. 48191 1995